TRANSPLANT OUTSIDE	T.L.C.	PROBLEMS	Incidentally
	Stake pole Beans, or plant near a Fence. Regular pinching prolongs harvest.	Don't harvest in the morning when Leaves are wet to reduce the chance of spreading diseases.	♡ Love the mixed... Yellow + purp... Be daring.. Try pl... outdoors 2 week...
Hardened off transplants tolerate some frost.	Cover with fine netting to keep out bugs (Row covers)	Cabbage Moth Larvae (yuck) eat and poop on uncovered Plants.	Cover for the Bugs. Cover SCHMOVER! I like varieties with small florets..so if bugs spoil some, there are Lots of others to pick from.
Ready?	Water + thin for Bigger Carrots. Avoid soils recently enriched with manure		Co-plant with radish to get the right spacing and prevent soil from crusting.
	Takes care of itself.		Love ♡ these to bits. Easy to grow enough for a household for a year.
Stagger transplanting to stagger harvest.		Becomes bitter quickly in Hot Weather... so Reseed regularly.	Am I Lazy or just forgetful? Mine go to seed then I remember I should have reseeded sooner.. Allow to self seed, saving time + feeding the gold finches.
	Use netting or chicken wire - or even branches - for climbing types.	Pick peas when plants are dry to minimize the spread of disease. Bunnies + Birds love seedlings.	These 2 peas are usually staking types - plant in cooler/shadier areas to prolong harvest.
Allow pieces to dry overnight or up to 2 Days. Dig a spade-deep hole in garden and place eye-side up.	Hill potatoes over growing season or cover with leaves as they grow to prevent green spuds.	Be wary... diseases ABOUND!	Many varieties now available... so mix it up. TRY something new Like BLUE
	KEEP RESEEDING	Flea Beetles on Leaves. Cracking from excess moisture.	Impress your friends by giving them seed pods in late summer after you forgot to pick roots and accidentally let the plants go to seed. Because it is so fast to mature, a good bedfellow for carrots, chard, beets.
Don't bother, just seed it directly.	Thin rows gradually to give more space to remaining plants	Leaf spot or Leaf miner, but just tear out damaged areas and cook	Buy multiple packets to get great colours, and better for you than beet tops. Young leaves great in salad; Large leaves great cooked.
1 week after frost.	Stake, tie, prune, primp, fertilize, water, Repeat!	Cutworms. Blossom end Rot. ALL kinds of blight + troubles but who cares? We want our TOMATOES!	Cherry-sized fruits actually taste better + Hybrid varieties often have more disease resistance. Forget the cherry tomatoes: Grow Beefsteaks for more bragging Rights

No Guff Vegetable Gardening

Donna M. Balzer & Steven A. Biggs

No Guff™ Vegetable Gardening

GROUP HUG

Our sincere thanks go out to:

Our fabulous group of "readers": friends and family who read early drafts, made helpful suggestions, and shared their opinions. You gave us great feedback and so much of your time—and you've helped us serve up a book that's been a lot of fun in the making. Our readers are Brennan Anderson, Shelley Biggs, Andrea DeKay, Jason Harris, Rodney McLean, Keith McCrae, Anne Newhouse, Susan Poizner, Peggy Proudfoot, Nicola Roe, Amie Silverwood, Melaine Van Loo, Margaret Webb, and Donna Young.

Christine Weber: your bookish instincts helped us improve our narrative and hone our tone.

David Cohlmeyer at Cookstown Greens walked his fields with us and gave us inspiring examples and encouragement.

Joan Altenhof for her support and hard work on our web page weather data.

Bryan and Mariko McCrae, the folks at Feedlot Studios created the look and feel of the book. Your charming drawings make us laugh Mariko–and that is a good thing!

Most importantly, we want to thank our spouses: Shelley Biggs and Keith McCrae. They helped on a daily basis with their humour and tolerance. Keith gave us much needed business advice and hands-on help with contracts and other business stuff.

He said) I am thankful to all the people who've infected me with a love of vegetable gardening, especially my parents Bob and Joanne; and my many gardening mentors including Joe Galleja, Anton and Edith Heinzle, Paul Mann, and Dimitrios Anapliotis.

Read more news and reviews at www.GardenCoachesChat.com, where coaches Balzer and Biggs give in-depth information to complement the book. Get a plan for a cold frame, look up Environment Canada's frost-free dates for your area, or read more about great succession crops. The companion website means you get more than a printed book: you get to dig deeper into topics that interest you.

For Keith,
DB

For Shelley, for nurturing me and the project.
SB

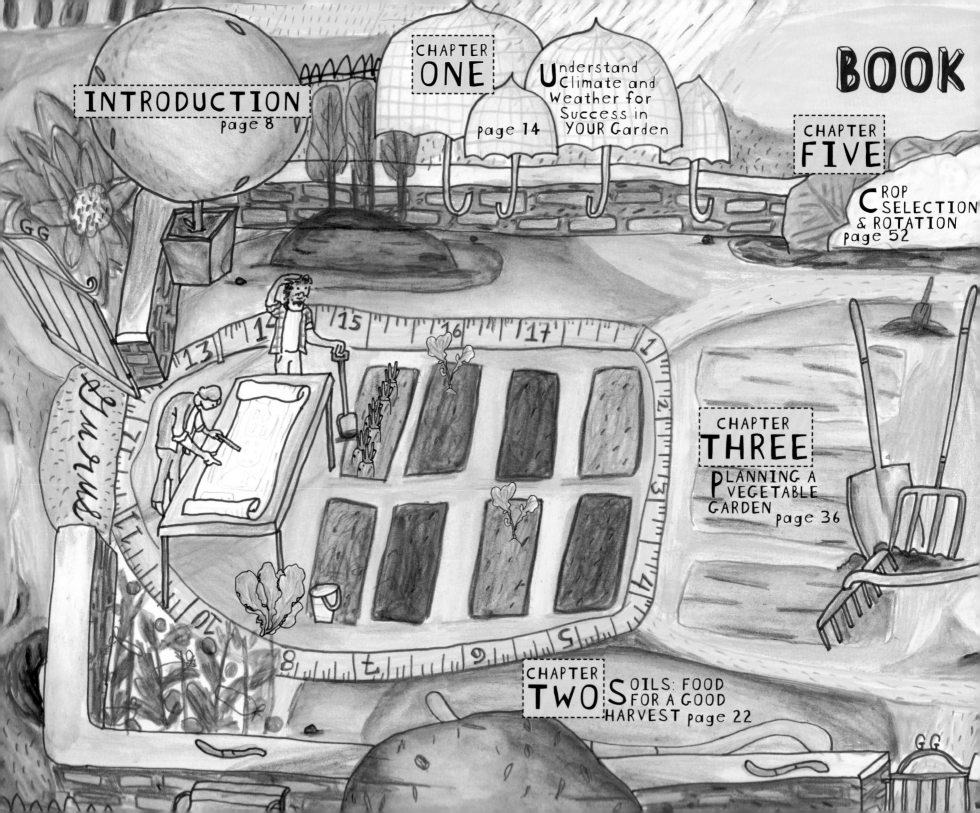

INTRODUCTION page 8

CHAPTER ONE Understand Climate and Weather for Success in YOUR Garden page 14

BOOK

CHAPTER FIVE Crop Selection & Rotation page 52

CHAPTER THREE Planning a Vegetable Garden page 36

CHAPTER TWO Soils: Food for a Good Harvest page 22

CONTENTS

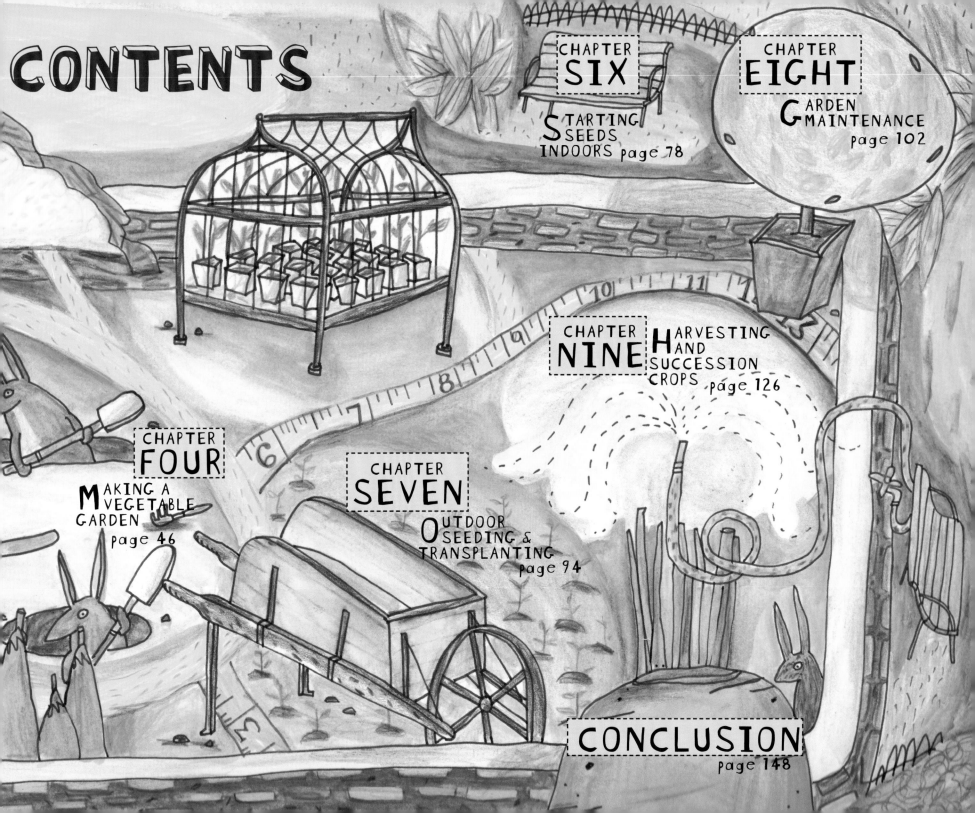

CHAPTER SIX

Starting Seeds Indoors page 78

CHAPTER EIGHT

Garden Maintenance page 102

CHAPTER NINE

Harvesting and Succession Crops page 126

CHAPTER FOUR

Making a Vegetable Garden page 46

CHAPTER SEVEN

Outdoor Seeding & Transplanting page 94

CONCLUSION page 148

INTRODUCTION:

GUFFAWS ABOUT GUFF

We Hope to Infect You

We both love to garden, and we both love growing vegetables. On game night, people married to hockey fans expect to lose their loved ones. Similarly, on weekends, Steve's wife, Shelley, and Donna's husband, Keith, expect to be gardening widow and widower.

As gardeners and writers, we hope to infect as many people as possible with a love of vegetable gardening. Sometimes, transmitting the gardening bug is easy, like when Donna gives extra tomato plants to boomer friends: she knows to expect glowing reports at harvest time. And Steve figures he's successfully infected his kids when his school-age daughter, Emma, demands a chunk of his vegetable garden—and when his toddler, Quinn, decides garden pathways make good roads for toy trucks and diggers.

Sometimes, the gardening bug needs help getting in the blood: the seed for this book was planted by Donna's stepdaughter, Heather, who phoned for a couple of quick veggie growing answers. Heather caught the gardening bug but was discouraged by garden bibles laced with theory, yet light on practical tips. It's a common approach: a Latin name, then some historical notes about civilizations that grew the vegetable. Once the reader has yawned through all that… there are prescriptive instructions with exact time frames, temperatures, dates, and spacing.

Our goal is simple: a more infectious model of writing about growing vegetables—one that provides easy access to information and lots of personal experience. We don't blather on about the sheer felicity of picking your own peas and carrots, like some sort of gardening glamour magazine.

Enjoy meeting our friends and family in our anecdotes. And meet our foil, Guff, who we've enlisted to help you spot questionable advice and products. The photos aren't perfect, and neither are we: We'll tell you about our failures, not just our successes in this serious, yet fun, look at vegetable gardening. When you're done, we're hoping you'll be incurably infected with a love of gardening, along with enough information and decision-making skills to give you fabulous results in your own garden.

We're the *Garden Coaches: No guff. Lots of fun.*

Introducing Guffaw

Guffaw: A loud, coarse burst of laughter.

Introducing Guff

Guff: Empty talk. Nonsense.

Ernie McGuff

Guff is the stuff you hope you're avoiding by buying a new gardening book or watching the latest TV gardening show.

Along with new guff, there's old guff that is reborn as new guff.

If you haven't wrapped your head around guff in the garden, think empty buzzwords; think pointless new products; think old theories passed off as new; and think about things that had you brimming with expectation…and let you down.

Introducing the Guffawers

About Donna and Guff

I once spent 50 dollars raising lettuce (several heads, mind you, more than I could ever use). I bought seed, paid rent on a garden plot, got some really cool garden stakes to mark rows, bought peat to loosen the soil, set up grow lights to get an early start indoors, and bought trays and cell packs.

I had a degree in agriculture and all of one minute of experience—and I wanted nothing but the best for my lettuce.

I still like to buy garden "stuff," to check out what is new, and to try every gadget or garden-related product at least once. When I find something that works, I suggest a product or idea to CBC listeners, readers, or consulting clients in Calgary.

About Steve and Guff

I got so charged up about the thieving rabbits that I once spent a ridiculous amount of money on an electric fence for my veggie patch. The fence worked… every time I touched it, but the rabbits hopped right through unawares.

Fence aside, I get used pots from friends and family, saving my gardening allowance for seeds and plants. In other words, I tend to be cheap, although, while collaborating with Donna, I occasionally have gadget envy.

I'm no stranger to the idea of spending money on growing supplies: I worked in the commercial horticultural supply industry amidst fertilizers and pesticides and equipment. But I think the home garden can be low input—and that's what I preach.

Donna Meets Steve

We studied agriculture at different universities at different times. Donna's a boomer—Steve's a Generation Xer.

On the surface, it might seem that we have only two things in common:

❀ We love gardening.

❀ We hate guff.

Donna and Steve's Thumbs-Up Guide

We like to give our thumbs up or down to guff and gardening stuff—and you'll see that throughout our book.

GUFF & GARDENING STUFF	DONNA	STEVE
Gardening	Up	Up
Guff	Down	Down
Gadgets	Up	Down
Cheap	Down	Up
Soil Friendly	Up	Up
Low Input	Up	Up
Simple	Up	Up

9

Why the Guffawers Guffaw About Guff

NOT BECAUSE We're Mean

We're not really mean people who like to laugh at other people. We prefer to laugh at ourselves.

NOT BECAUSE We're Terribly Opinionated

While we have opinions about vegetable gardening, we're not normally uber-opinionated people. We like to chat and listen.

BECAUSE Success in the Veggie Patch Is Really, Really Fun

We love the garden and want everyone to enjoy it as we do, without wasting money or falling for hokey methods.

BECAUSE Our Chosen Field Suffers When People Give Up on Gardening.

With some first-hand gardening insight, anybody can make solid gardening decisions and succeed.

BECAUSE a Filter Helps

We get vegetable gardening: it's our game...and we spot exaggerated or suspicious claims. That makes us the right people to guffaw for you.

What's to Guffaw About?

* Pointless commercial products.
* Questionable home remedies.
* Unrealistic practices.
* Baseless over-the-fence tips.
* Greenwashed commercial products.
* Greenwashed techniques.
* Impractical theories that make sense only on a large scale.
* What sounds to us like bad advice or misguided ideas.

And, yes, we sometimes guffaw (kind-heartedly) at each other!

Our Guff-Busting Advice to You

Three words: JUST ASK WHY.

* Why does this work?
* Why do I need it?
* Why is it right for the home vegetable garden?

Some Favourite Guffaws

Guff Says

Test the soil before you do anything else...even if you haven't got a clue what you are looking for.

GUFFAWERS RESPOND

Maybe there's one in your family, the hypochondriac forever afflicted by—or seeking—some sort of health ailment and popping an endless stream of prescriptions.

Here's our prescription: don't be a soil hypochondriac. Skip the laboratory soil test.

Why do we say this?

* A meaningful test is based on a good sample. Soil is often highly disturbed in home gardens, meaning the soil in one bed could be entirely different from the soil in the next bed.

* Striving for optimal nutrient values in the soil is an act of perfectionism—and a waste of time. You'll know your soil best by growing crops in it. A printout showing numbers and percentages does little for the average gardener.

The best test of your soil is to grow a garden. Grow one—and tend it well—for two or three seasons. If it's reasonably productive, keep gardening.

After this "dating period," if you are not getting good results, consider a test.

Still can't shake the desire to test your soil?

Instead of paying for expensive and complex soil tests, try a home bioassay (explained on page 28).

When do we think an immediate laboratory soil test makes sense?

If you're gardening on what was formerly industrial land and are worried about industrial contaminants in the soil, a laboratory test is a good idea.

We repeat: We think the must-do-a-soil-test mentality is guff and we aren't alone.

"I direct home gardeners to take the money they would have spent on a soil test and use that to buy compost or fertilizer," says John Paul, soil chemist with 28 years as a soil-testing professional. He adds, "I am a firm believer in good soil structure for plant growth. A soil test for a home gardener is a waste of money. To me, the important thing is soil structure."

Guff Says

Soaker hoses and drip hoses are a "must" for environmentally minded gardeners.

WHAT ABOUT LOAM?

Loam is often the lay term used to describe heavenly soil. Only dachshunds have the genetic ingredients for dachshund puppies, and only certain soils have the ingredients (called parent material) for loam. A loam is thought by many to be the ideal blend of ingredients, with balanced proportions of soil building blocks called sand, silt, and clay (see page 24). But… not many soils are true loams: it is one of only 12 types of soil texture possible. Loam is very nice for vegetable gardening, but few of us have it.

GUFFAWERS RESPOND

Nope.

Having each replaced a good number of such hoses over time, we question how innocuous all that waste hose is. And we've had enough leaky drip hoses that flood one part of the garden while leaving another dry that we're both lukewarm to drip hoses.

Overhead watering has its virtues: simple technology, long lasting, and less chance of leaving plants and microbes thirsty. It can also wash off a few bugs.

Guff Says

Buy good loam.

GUFFAWERS RESPOND

This is like saying you really want a purebred dachshund puppy from a Labrador-cross mother. Impossible.

So why do gardeners keep advising other gardeners to buy good loam? Do these guff pushers realize they are setting an impossible standard? Really, if your soil is a sandy-clay texture, there is no possible way you will ever change it to loam. If you live in a region where all soils are the same texture—and not loam—how in the world are you even going to buy "loam" at any price?

Donna and Steven suggest you become intimate with your soil. Do a hand texture test. Feel it. Smell it. Then amend it so that it grows great crops. Simple.

Latin names make sense for flowers (top *Calendula officinalis*, bottom *Tagetes patula*) but not vegetables.

Guff Says

Master those Latin plant names.

GUFFAWERS RESPOND

Latin schmatin. Pass the *Cucurbita pepo* might get you a blank stare from both Steve and Donna. Linnaeus gave us a great system—the Latin binomial—as a way to classify plants and animals and avoid confusingly similar "common" names.

Take the case of the common names for two common annual flowers, pot marigold and French marigold. Both are often called marigold, even though their uses and appearance are quite different. Gardeners can talk about them using their Latin names to avoid confusion: the former is Calendula officinalis, while the latter is Tagetes patula. No doubt these two are different.

Here's the guff: Latin is more useful for flowers. Take Cucurbita pepo: it applies to pumpkins, summer squash, spaghetti squash, and acorn squash. The Latin name doesn't distinguish the plant we stuff with breadcrumbs and grate for chocolate cake from the one we cut up for jack-o-lanterns.

Latin names are a waste of breath in the veggie garden, so you won't see them used here.

Guff Says

Growing your own vegetables will save the world.

GUFFAWERS RESPOND

Don't get us wrong: Knowing how to grow your own food is a great thing. If you're serious about it, you can save money. And if you get kids in on the act, they not only understand where food comes from—they'll probably nibble some garden vegetables too.

But for most people, home vegetable gardening is not about saving money or the world. It's about enjoying fresh food—and understanding what goes into growing it. It's the earliest spud of the season or the still-warm tomato straight from the vine that really make it rewarding. By the time you outfit yourself with supplies and expend energy to grow some cool tomatoes, we suggest you're probably not having a big effect on your carbon footprint compared to buying a vine-ripened tomato from afar.

So go ahead, be a tree-hugging, heirloom-munching, organic-and-sustainable low-carbon-footprint garden geek. Even throw in some unbridled locavorism. But seriously, you're not saving the world.

Guff Says

Organic fertilizer is always better than conventional.

GUFFAWERS RESPOND

Sure, if you want industrialized perfection, fertilizer—including organic products—might just do the trick. But seriously, if you're interested in the idea of organics, shouldn't you be shunning the pursuit of picture-perfect food?

Forget about comparing organic fertilizers to inorganic or conventional fertilizers: they are all external commercial products. They all require energy for manufacturing, packaging, and shipping, when soil nutrition can often be managed without them.

Are all commercial products bad? No. But you might not need them.

It's easy to buy a product that fixes symptoms but doesn't get to the heart of the matter. Instead, first energize the garden with nutrients locked up in the safety deposit box of organic matter and microbes.

She said When I buy products of any kind, I look for the OMRI symbol. It gives me a sense of reassurance and reduces my research time. I find it interesting that organic standards vary so widely. In England, bone meal and other animal by-products are no longer considered suitable for organic production. I like that.

WHAT IS ORGANIC?

Organic Matter

The word organic technically describes something that contains carbon. When we talk about adding organic matter to the garden, we're talking about things such as composted leaves—which contain carbon.

Organic Gardening

Organic gardening first and foremost improves soil by building up organic matter. When it comes to agriculture and gardening, organic production generally refers to growing without synthetic fertilizers and pesticides.

Certified Organic

Certified organic means a certifying body has said, "This product meets our organic standards." An example of a certifying body is the Organic Materials Review Institute (OMRI), an organization that prescribes products allowed for use in organic production. It is used widely in both Canada and the United States.

He said Why no bone meal, Donna—are your plants vegetarian?

I'm always curious to see if I get a strained look when I say I'm leery of the word organic—it's like digging in sacred ground. Here's why I avoid the term: It means different things to different people. Some people think it means no pesticides—but that's not always the case. Some people associate it with sustainable agriculture—but I see enough mass-produced, imported, and highly packaged "organic" salad greens to doubt that. I never look for the word organic when I shop for garden supplies. I'd rather buy a good product, one that's produced locally—organic or not.

Guff Says
Always buy "natural" products first.

GUFFAWERS RESPOND

At risk of tarnishing good products with the bad, we suggest a bit of due diligence when someone tries to sell you on "natural" or homemade remedies.

Many are good. Some are far, far from benign.

He said It started with me husking black walnuts to dry for winter. Having husked the walnuts, I thought I'd give them a quick swish in a pail of water to rinse off some of the hand-staining juice remaining on the shells. But when I dumped out that rinse water on my lawn, worms—lots of worms—came writhing to the surface nearly immediately. And they all died. Walnuts are natural—

and the ones I was husking were organically grown…zero inputs. But they sure are toxic to worms.

Guff Says
Borax for your ants…it's harmless.

GUFFAWERS RESPOND

Used properly, borax works well for ants. No argument there. But…some guff pushers fail to point out that you DON'T want this stuff on your soil.

Donna was called in to help a mother who was hosting her daughter's wedding party in her backyard. The mom did not want a single ant bothering a single guest—and, having read that borax and sugar mixed in equal parts would kill ants—used it liberally around the yard.

The mother read the caution to keep it away from children and pets, but didn't have pets nor did she expect children at the wedding.

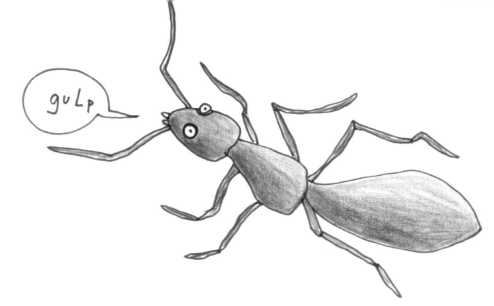

What she wanted was flowers—lots of them.

Too bad, because what she didn't know was that borax affects more than just ants: it can kill plants too—and should be kept away from desirable plants, shrubs, trees, and grasses.

Poor mom, she was unable to grow anything in her garden for the wedding!

Guff Grows
Look for more guff at the end of every chapter, and on our website, www.GardenCoachesChat.com.

Have some guff you want to share? We'd love to guffaw at it too—visit our website and drop us a line.

Garden Coaches Chat: No guff. Lots of fun.
for more details visit www.GardenCoachesChat.com

13

Understand Climate and Weather for Success in YOUR Garden

You're probably wondering why we begin a book about No Guff vegetable gardening with a section on climate and weather. Even if you're bored by talk of rain, sun, wind, and temperatures, don't skip this chapter!

The reason is simple: heat, water, and sunlight are key ingredients in any successful vegetable garden. If you understand the relationship between these factors and your vegetable crops, you get an edge as a gardener.

In your own little piece of the world, you may be on a hill battered by winds, in a sheltered site, or living beside the ocean or in a frost-prone valley. Instead of memorizing your zone, we suggest that you think more about the day-to-day weather in your own backyard.

ZONE MAPS

Zone maps are intended to give you the big picture of what grows where. But zone maps are like painting with a large paintbrush on a small canvas: many fine details are left out. Zone maps shouldn't be top priority for vegetable gardeners: they apply more to trees, shrubs, and perennials than they do to annual vegetables.

Frost: Why it Matters

Frost matters to vegetable gardeners. But more than a destructive force, gardeners use knowledge of frost for planning:

※ The average last spring frost date is important for vegetable gardeners because it is the milepost that helps us decide when to plant seeds indoors and in the garden.

※ The date of the average first fall frost is important too: More than the curtain falling at the end of the summer show, it allows us to gauge how many frost-free growing days we have—something that is important to know when choosing crop varieties. Some tomato varieties, for example, are ready in 60 days, while others take 85 days. The difference of 25 days is a big deal in an area with a short frost-free period.

Don't restrict yourself to published first- and last-frost dates. Talk to other gardeners in the area to find out what dates they use—because your microclimate might be unique. Check out our weather data on www.GardenCoachesChat.com.

More than crystals on a leaf, frost is a planning tool for gardeners.

Frost Hardy

arugula, asparagus, broccoli, Brussels sprouts, cabbage, Chinese cabbage, cress, garlic, kale, kohlrabi, leaf lettuce, leeks, onions and related crops, parsley, parsnip, radish, rhubarb, peas, sage, spinach, turnip

Semi Frost Hardy

asparagus pea, beet, cardoon, carrot, cauliflower, celery, chard, endive, fennel, head lettuce, potatoes

Frost Tender

basil, bean, cilantro (coriander), corn, cucumber, eggplant, muskmelon (a.k.a. cantaloupe), okra, pepper, pumpkin, winter and summer squash (a.k.a zucchini and courgette), tomato, watermelon

He said I remember my grandfather in Calgary (my Dido), Peter Konachowicz, successfully nurtured tomato plants through Calgary's tottery spring weather using a bank of permanent cold frames that stretched across the back of the garden. I can still picture that garden—in a backyard that boasted more vegetable garden than grass in an era when grass reigned supreme. While most memories of toddlerhood are hazy, I can clearly picture Baba hobbling down the stairs of the back laundry stoop, alternately scolding me and wagging her finger after I pulled a carrot from the garden. No harm done: it didn't deter me.

She said With an average 112 frost-free days in summer, Calgary gets fewer frost-free nights per year than most gardens in Canada but not as few as Nordegg, Alberta (46 days) or Kapuskasin, Ontario (86 days).

The key messages about frost are:

❋ Frost is not the same as sustained freezing temperatures.

❋ Frost doesn't always blanket the landscape in a uniform fashion.

❋ Many tender plants suffer "cold-temperature injury" even if temperatures don't dip below freezing.

❋ Killing frost is colder than light frost.

KILLING FROST

While light frost may injure leaves, a killing frost kills entire plants. Cold tolerance varies by species—so a killing frost for one crop may not kill another. In general, people use the term killing frost to talk about prolonged, below-freezing spells that shut down the vegetable garden for winter or kills plants outright in spring.

Frost: Not Just Freezing Temperatures

Many people think of frost as textured, white crystals that appear overnight on grass, roofs, and windows.

For gardeners, a frost warning means temperatures that dip near or slightly below the freezing point. If "near" sounds imprecise, that's the point we want to drive home: forecasting the weather is not an exact science. In most landscapes, there are conditions that help some gardens to escape frost, while in others there are frost pockets—places where cold air is trapped against the ground and unable to flow away.

Frost Hardiness

Tomato plants are frost-tender—they hate cold. That's why Steve's Dido had cold frames to protect them from the unpredictable Calgary spring. In the same way that some people feel the cold more than others do, some plants feel it more too. A mere sniff of cold, something as seemingly tropical as +5 C (41 F), will incite protest in the basil patch, where brimming plants droop in protest and drop leaves. Treat a zucchini or eggplant to such a temperature…and there will be protest in those ranks too. At least cold-sensitive people can slip into a sweater!

❋ **Frost-hardy** vegetable plants can survive a few degrees of frost and are usually the first varieties planted in the garden in early spring.

Zucchini protest: tender plants droop even when temperatures are above freezing.

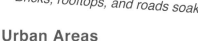
She said When there's a spring frost warning, I use row covers—which look like the fabric softener sheets used in the dryer—and binder clips from the office to cover plants and create a microclimate. The clips keep the fabric wrapped around the sensitive plants, giving frost protection. Some years we play dress-up like this until mid-June!

Bricks, rooftops, and roads soak up and radiate heat.

Hardy doesn't mean unkillable: hardy plants might not tolerate frost if they've just been moved outside from warm, snug conditions under grow lights. But they do gradually adapt and, once "hardened off" (see page 98), can sail through light frosts in the fall.

❀ **Semi-frost-hardy** plants, while less tolerant of cold than frost-hardy crops, can often be sown almost as early as frost-hardy crops because they germinate slowly in cold soil.

❀ **Frost-tender** crops are damaged or killed by frost and set back by temperatures of +5 C (41 F) or lower.

Microclimates

A microclimate exists where the climate is different from the surrounding area. Some microclimates occur naturally, while others are artificially created.

As a vegetable gardener, understanding local microclimatic factors—and even creating your own microclimate—helps you achieve an EARLIER harvest.

Bodies of Water

Gardens next to large bodies of water often have a more moderate climate than adjacent areas. This occurs because water heats up and cools down more slowly than air, giving lakeside and maritime regions cooler spring temperatures and warmer fall temperatures.

While they may not be very noticeable to us, such slight temperature differences can be good news for vegetable plants: cooler spring temperatures can allow time for plants to become established before summertime blast-furnace temperatures set in. In the fall, when the first frost is delayed by a few days, there is more time for crops to mature.

He said Here in Toronto, gardeners know that if you live close to Lake Ontario, you can often escape that first fall frost. But when spring rolls around, gardeners close to the lake have to wait a bit longer for the tulips to bloom.

Urban Areas

When you think about all the asphalt soaking up solar heat in urban areas—and all the buildings giving off heat—it's no surprise that urban areas are often slightly warmer than nearby rural areas.

He said I use the hot microclimate on my garage roof for heat-loving crops such as melon and eggplant. They're leaps and bounds ahead of siblings at ground level.

Elevation and Latitude

It might sound counterintuitive, but northerly areas sometimes have a longer frost-free period than areas to the south. This happens when the northerly area has a lower elevation. For example, Edmonton is 668 metres (2191 feet) above sea level while Calgary is 1048 metres (3437 feet). Even though Edmonton is 300 km (186 miles) further north, it has almost 30 more frost-free days than Calgary.

Latitude, the distance from the equator, also affects microclimate. Grande Prairie, Alberta, is at almost the same elevation as Edmonton but is 465 km (288 miles) northwest. Being farther north, it gets longer days in the summer—and those longer days are great for intensive veggie growth.

Around the Vegetable Garden

A walled vegetable garden is a good example of a garden microclimate: plants beside a south-facing stone or brick wall enjoy extra heat radiated by the wall. Similarly, when a garden is on a slope, cold air can "roll" off—while a garden that is in a low-lying area can trap cold air and be touched by frost before higher surrounding areas.

In rural settings, gardeners can make use of solar reflection off a barn, garage, or home to heat up a small area for heat-loving veggies.

He said

Recently I made a new veggie plot in a partially shaded area, under an old apple tree. The shade makes this garden cooler in the summer. It's more suitable for crops such as lettuce and spinach, which do poorly in the heat.

She said

A client asked if it is better to paint a garden wall white (for increased reflection) or black (for increased heat absorption). It depends on the site. If the area is shady but warm at night use light coloured materials or paint the wall white for increased light. In a cooler climate, where there is plenty of light, darker walls will absorb heat and warm the air and soil.

Make Your Own Crop-Boosting Microclimate

We said we would give you a primer on weather and climate because they are important to the vegetable gardener. Here comes the practical stuff: the ideas for making a microclimate to give your vegetable plants a head start. Try some of these and your patience and effort could be mistaken for gardening genius.

Cold Frame

A cold frame is nothing more than a simple mini-greenhouse heated by the sun. In its simplest form, it can be an old window set atop sides made from boards (or even straw bales).

My Dad, Bob, had an open-backed cold frame that he set up in front of a basement window. On cold nights, he left the window open to keep the temperature in the cold frame above freezing.

A greenhouse allows gardeners an early start.

A cold frame is simply a mini greenhouse heated by the sun.

Be creative: old hospital lights as cloches!

Cloches and Hotcaps

Using cloches (also known as hotcaps) is one way to use the cold-frame concept on a smaller scale. In past times glass blowers created fabulous glass bells—cloches—to keep plants warm overnight. The modern equivalent is an empty milk jug or pop bottle with the bottom cut out. The cap can be removed to allow the hotcap to cool down during the day. They're ideal for spring, but not great once temperatures soar…as they can cook the plants inside.

One spring, when I was much younger, I used cloches to protect my tomatoes from frost, and finally removed them on June 8. That night the temperature dropped to -8 C (18 F). The moral of the story? Tools are no better than the gardener using them!

Cold frames serve three purposes for the vegetable gardener:

* Provide a warm spot to grow seedling transplants while it is still too cold outside.

* Protect early in-ground crops of greens such as lettuce, arugula, and spinach while the ground outside is still frozen.

* Shelter fall crops of greens.

Ideally, the cold frame faces south, with the back wall slightly higher than the front, so that the window is on a slope to catch more sunlight.

Because it is heated by the sun, it cools down when the sun sets, though it doesn't become as cool as the surrounding garden. That's because a cold frame

also traps some of the heat given off by the ground. Covering it with a blanket or tarp on very cold nights will keep it slightly warmer.

On warm, sunny days a cold frame can actually become too hot, so it is important to prop open the window to let out some of the heat (or invest in automatic vents). Visit www.GardenCoachesChat.com for a simple cold frame plan.

MAGGI'S TOMATO MICROCLIMATE FOR CALGARY

Donna's friend Maggi uses hardware wire and plastic sheeting to get better tomato crops in the unpredictable Calgary weather. She shapes the wire into a hoop around the plants and cuts harvesting holes in the wire. Then she surrounds the whole works with plastic and, using clothes pegs, attaches the plastic loosely to the wire frame. This allows her to plant outside a few weeks earlier than Donna. When the days are sunny and warm, she opens the top. At night she uses the pegs to keep it closed.

Maggi's magic kit for early tomatoes: wire mesh and plastic.

Hotbed

Avid gardeners can take the cold-frame concept and turbo-charge it to get an extra early start, while there's still snow on the ground. All you need is a cold frame with a source of heat underneath. This combination of cold frame and heat is called a hotbed.

Seed greens in a hotbed before spring arrives.

18

The traditional method calls for unrotted horse manure to be placed in a hole, and then capped with a layer of soil. The manure gives off heat as it breaks down, heating the soil from underneath.

Excavate the pit in the fall, so there's no need to chisel through frozen ground. Set aside a couple tubs of the soil, ready to cap the manure when the hotbed is started in late winter.

Squeamish about poo? Or worried about the microbes that come with it? Electric heating cables are a microbe-free heating alternative.

IS THAT POO FRESH?

Fresh, unrotted manure is what is needed to power a hotbed because it has the potential to give off heat as it breaks down. In the case of horse manure—the Cadillac manure of the hotbed world—little round balls of poo are a pretty good indication it hasn't broken down into uniform compost. Bagged manure from garden centres is not fresh and will not produce heat.

Compost Pile

Composting kitchen and yard waste is back in vogue. Along with creating a nutrient-packed amendment for vegetable garden soil, composting offers gardeners something else too: a warm spot for growing.

The concept is simple. Put a layer of soil over an immature compost pile and plant into it. The soil is gently heated from below with heat generated as leaves and kitchen scraps decompose.

You're probably wondering how to add new scraps or leaves to the composter when you're growing crops on it. You don't. Instead, have an active composter, to which you're adding new stuff, as well as a full one. That full one serves temporarily as a garden.

Steve gathers fresh horse manure for his hotbed in February.

Dark containers in a sunny spot provide a warm microclimate for heat-loving crops.

Containers

In-ground gardeners take note: don't dismiss containers! They're not just for patio and balcony gardeners. They speed up crops and are especially good for heat-loving plants such as okra and eggplant.

Containers work well for a few reasons:

- The soil in containers (especially dark ones that absorb sunlight) warms up more quickly than the ground.
- Containers can be moved around to grab the most sunlight possible.
- Unlike garden beds, you choose the soil that goes into the container.

Unheated Greenhouses and Tunnels

An unheated greenhouse or tunnel can take vegetable garden climate manipulation to the next level. They're not warmer than a cold frame (unless heat is added) but can be made bigger. When the sun is shining, they trap heat from sunlight and

Row covers protect plants from light frost in spring and fall.

become warmer than neighbouring parts of the garden. At night, as the air temperature drops, these covered areas remain slightly warmer as they hold in heat given off by the ground.

Tunnels are useful for three to four weeks and can be removed as the plants grow and outdoor temperatures increase. Like cold frames, unheated greenhouses and tunnels can benefit from an overnight cover when spring temperatures are cool.

Visit www.GardenCoachesChat.com for simple instructions on how to make your own tunnel.

She said Decide what you want to grow under a tunnel before you buy supplies such as pipe or wire.

"FLOATING" ROW COVERS

You may see the term floating row covers—a description that can give new gardeners images of sorcery in the garden.

Nothing's really floating: it's just that the row cover is unsupported, as compared to the tunnels where the row cover fabric lies on top of arched wire or flexible plastic tubing. A floating row cover lies right on the vegetables, actually touching the plants—but it is light enough not to crush them.

He said The theory behind fabric row covers is great. But I don't use them much... simply don't have time.

Heated Greenhouse

A heated greenhouse is the ultimate climate enhancer…but that's a whole other book.

Visit www.GardenCoachesChat.com for our advice on greenhouses.

She said After several years of ripening tomatoes on the basement floor, I eventually got a greenhouse that my daughter let me put up in her Calgary yard. When she moved away, I had to take apart my greenhouse and move it to my B.C. garden where I have a bigger yard. Ironically, I now have to listen to people in B.C. complain about the short tomato season on the West Coast.

Climate Guff Busted

Guff Says
Don't plant beans until after the last frost date.

GUFFAWERS RESPOND

Sure, bush, dry, and pole beans hate cold. But if you wait until after the last frost date, you're losing potential yield.

Plant a "cheater" row of seeds a week or two before the last frost date. If the seeds germinate and poke up without being nipped by frost, you're ahead of the game. If they are hit by frost, you've lost nothing more than some seed, and simply reseed.

Donna's greenhouse: a warm microclimate for tomatoes and basil in cold cold Calgary.

Guff Says

You're always better off as a gardener to live further south.

GUFFAWERS RESPOND

The argument seems to make sense, but elevation and day length mean that it's never that simple.

She said Everyone jokes about gardening in a high elevation or far northern latitude, but when I gardened up north in Grande Prairie, once the snow was gone the long days made up the growing difference. I grew corn there even though I have never successfully grown it in Calgary.

Real Vegetable Gardeners Don't...

Real vegetable gardeners don't take frost warnings lightly. Instead, they protect heat-loving crops.

Summary: Climate, Weather, and Success in the Garden

Success growing vegetable plants hinges on giving plants the light and heat they need.

Don't think too much about zones: instead, focus on tweaking your microclimate to increase your harvest and have success with crops that don't normally do well in your area.

Donna and Steve's Thumbs-Up Guide

GUFF & GARDENING STUFF	DONNA	STEVE
Row Covers	Up	Down
Cold Frames	Up	Up

Garden Coaches Chat: No guff. Lots of fun.
for more details visit www.GardenCoachesChat.com

2

SOILS: FOOD FOR A GOOD HARVEST

DEFINITIONS

Soil: The stuff that's so important to a good vegetable garden that we stuck it at the front of the book.

Mulch: A covering placed over the soil to hold in moisture and modify soil temperature.

Amendment: Something mixed in with the soil to improve or change its properties.

Steve wasn't fast enough! He saw his toddler Quinn raise a hand to his mouth, but Quinn knew that he had been caught in the act...and quickly stuck his hand in his mouth to have his first taste of...soil.

Toddlers love to taste everything. I figured the soil wouldn't taste good and he wouldn't bother eating it again. But sure enough, I was wrong and he had another taste of it a couple of days later, beaming up at me as he wiped a large, dark smudge of soil across his cheeks.

He said

While most people—toddlers excepted—don't eat soil, it is nourishing stuff: it feeds your vegetable plants, along with things we can't see, such as bacteria, fungi, protozoans, and nematodes (see page 119). All these too-small-to-be-seen dinner guests decompose, mix, and redistribute the nutrients in soil, which in turn makes it a veritable buffet for our vegetable plants.

Top 3 Sensible Soil Tips

1. Take off your gloves, touch the soil, and become familiar with the feel of it.

2. Make soil improvement an ongoing process. It's better than buying "new" soil.

3. Think of soil building like muscle building: good soil gives strength (in numbers of microbes) and gives plants more get-up-and-go.

CHECKLIST FOR HEALTHY SOIL

❀ Warms well in spring

❀ Soft to the touch and easy to dig

❀ No obvious crusting on soil surface

❀ Nice structure with clods that crumble apart into smaller soft pieces when crushed by hand

❀ Not too sticky or gummy when wet

❀ Holds moisture in dry spells

Recipe for Yummy Soil

Ingredients:
- Rock
- Living stuff
- Weather

Preparation Instructions:
- Leave rock outdoors for a few thousand years to allow it to be pulverized by the force of freezing water, consumed by algae, chiselled by tree roots, sandblasted by wind, eroded by waves and glaciers, and worn down by rushing rivers.

- Next, leave the now-pulverized rock a few thousand more years so that living stuff such as plants and animals will die on it and get mixed in.

Serving Ideas:
- Give to garden plants with a healthy dollop of bacteria.
- Garnish with fungi.

Soil: What You See

Digesting the Importance of Organic Matter

"Organic matter is what organic farming is all about," David Cohlmeyer told us as we toured his market garden, Cookstown Greens, north of Toronto. Cohlmeyer makes no bones about his thoughts on soil organic matter: it is the central tenet of organic production—and a soil rich in it makes for plants with good pest and disease resistance.

Not quite sure what the term organic matter encompasses? In our yummy soil recipe we talk about the living stuff such as plants and animals that die and get mixed in with the soil. That's it—that's organic matter. And while we're on living stuff, don't forget the living stuff we don't see…all the microbes. When they kick the bucket, they become organic matter too.

Here's all the science you need to know for now: they all contain carbon. That's as scientific as we gardeners need to get. Dead stuff that has carbon is what makes organic matter.

Soil Organic Matter: Like Eggs in Baking

Leaf through any baking recipe and you'll see a call for eggs. The reason is simple: eggs play a key role in the structure of the baked good—binding, giving strength, and adding moisture.

When cooking up a good soil, organic matter is a critical ingredient. It helps bind together the pulverized rock bits we talk about in our soil recipe. While it's binding them, though, it's also spacing them out—which is good, because the bits can settle together closely, leaving little room for air and water. And that's a problem—because plants require air and water in soil.

Organic matter leavens the soil, adding air pockets, while at the same time binding together the various pieces and retaining moisture.

23

Organic Matter and Microbes

Beyond the physical structure, organic matter is the dormitory for all those partying microbes in the soil—the guys that are busy eating the organic matter, eating each other, and getting cosy with plant roots, maybe even sharing some extra nutrients.

Not all organic matter is equal when it comes to microbes. Peat comes from a fairly sterile environment (acidic conditions without air), so it's pretty sterile to begin with. Fresh animal manure comes packed with microbes...but along with the good ones, there are bad ones that we don't really want in our vegetable garden.

Composting is the process that prepares organic matter for the garden. Part of the preparation is shifting the microbial balance.

> **He said**
>
> When I first teamed up with Donna, I, too, had a passion for soil organic matter. And I believed in the role of microbes as decomposers. After all, I added compost religiously to my soil every year. But I thought she went overboard with her sorcery of compost teas and what seemed to me like an infatuation with soil microbes.
>
> I still don't make compost tea—have enough trouble stopping to make myself a coffee—but as we've talked about our ideas, I've become more pumped about soil microbes.

> **She said**
>
> I have learned to look at my soil under a microscope to see what I've got-how many fungi, bacteria, and protozoans there are. It's really exciting, like a garden diary for my soil.

Pets are another species that lives with us, providing either companionship or some sort of work. In return, we feed our pets. Plants have their own sort of pets: mycorrhizae—a type of fungus—colonize plant roots. They eat plant-supplied food and, in return, help plants retrieve the nutrients they need from the soil...like a pet dog fetching a stick.

Soil Textures: Think Genres

Maybe we're stretching things a bit to compare soil to music. But consider rock music: to people uninterested in it, it probably all sounds mostly the same. But to those who love it, the genre encompasses an amazing variety of sub-genres such as soft rock, glam rock, hard rock, punk rock, heavy metal, alternative rock—and probably more still (we don't claim to be music experts).

When we talk about soil, we don't talk about genres and sub-genres: we talk about "textures." With a whopping 12 textures forming the backbone of the soil classification system, you might say that soil science is an art.

Particle Size: The Backbone of Soil Textures

This quick walk through the world of soil classification will give you enough of an idea about soil types so that you can make smart soil decisions for your vegetable garden. We'll start with the size of those little bits of pulverized rocks in our soil recipe:

SOIL TRIANGLE

Blend the rock bits in different amounts and you'll get different textures. The soil triangle classifies soils into textures based on the relative proportions of sand, silt, and clay.

Each texture has benefits. Soils with a lot of sand drain well and warm up quickly in the spring, while clay- and silt-based soils hold more nutrients and moisture. But there are disadvantages too: Clay can form hard clods when dry, while sand dries out quite quickly. The way water behaves in different soils is different too: it percolates in (and out) of sandy soils very quickly, making frequent watering a requirement. Clay and silt soils, on the other hand, tend to stay wet a long time after a rain.

ROCK BITS	RELATIVE SIZE	COOKING EQUIVALENCY
Sand	Largest particles	Sand is the large chunks of potato and carrot in a stew.
Clay	Mid-sized particles	Clay is the peppercorns.
Silt	Smallest particles	Silt is the fine cornstarch used to thicken the gravy.

WHAT IS HEAVY SOIL?

A soil with 40 to 100 per cent clay is described as "heavy." This soil can be sticky and hard to turn.

Don't Sweat Soil Texture

There's a good chance that the soil triangle will show you that you don't have a loam soil. That's fine. In the veggie garden, the main thing to remember is that you can amend your soil so that it has better drainage and water-holding capabilities—even if it's not the ideal texture. It's rare to have perfect soil—and highly impractical (and expensive) to replace it.

Don't try to add sand or a different soil on top of what you have: at the end of the day the same texture is still there underneath.

A CAKE HALF BAKED

Soils found in the mountains, in the far north, and some coastal islands might not be as well developed as soils in other areas. Instead, these half-baked soils are still forming, so consist largely of coarse particles of gravel and sand and drain quickly. Like fully formed soils, they definitely benefit from the addition of organic matter.

What To Do If You Have...

Below are some of the soil texture types found in the soil triangle. Not sure how to manage your soil if it's one of the types we list below? For us, it's simple: add organic matter and encourage microbial activity.

Organic matter can "lighten" a heavy clay soil, while giving an overly drained sandy soil the ability to retain more water.

SOIL TYPE	DO ✓	DON'T ✗
Clay	Do add organic matter.	Don't compact it by working it or walking on it when it's wet.
	Do encourage microbial activity.	
Clay Loam	Do add organic matter.	Don't compact it by working it or walking on it when it's wet.
	Do encourage microbial activity.	
Sand	Do add organic matter.	Don't water as infrequently as clay soils.
	Do encourage microbial activity.	
Sandy Loam	Do add organic matter.	Don't water as infrequently as clay soils.
	Do encourage microbial activity.	
Loam	Do add organic matter.	Don't take it for granted. Keep up the organic matter levels.
	Do encourage microbial activity.	
Silty Loam	Do add organic matter.	Don't walk on it when wet—it is slippery.
	Do encourage microbial activity.	
I have no idea what I have!	Do add organic matter.	Don't worry. You don't have to be a soil scientist to garden.
	Do encourage microbial activity.	

The texture of even an ideal loam doesn't give the whole picture about its suitability for growing plants. It may have what can cause hypertension in humans—high salts (see page 122)—or it may have a really sour disposition (see Sweet and Sour, page 26). And it may have really high or really low amounts of organic matter. So think of texture as a starting point—just one element of great soil.

CLAY ISN'T A DEMON

Here in Toronto I garden on clay. I hear gardeners lament the fact that they have clay soil—as if it's a curse.

He said

I disagree. In fact, I've added clay to the garden. When I took out part of my driveway to make more garden, I ordered a load of soil. Unfortunately, I didn't ask enough questions, and ended up with a load of black fluffy stuff. It was nutrient-rich, but had very little water-holding capacity. So I took some of the clay I was excavating from another part of the yard and I added it to that light, fluffy soil to give it better water and nutrient holding capacity.

My sandy-silt soil was so dusty and dry the neighbourhood quail used it for dust baths. It was also low in nutrients, which leached away. Clay is a dream! At least you can amend it, and it holds water and nutrients.

She said

You Don't See The Half Of It!

Fungi, one branch of soil microbes, set up shop in the roots of some plants. Once there, they help plants take up nutrients and help suppress disease. Some researchers figure fungi account for up to 50 per cent of the microbial mass in soil.

Aside from helping plants, the other thing they do is improve the soil by creating an "aggregate" structure.

AGGREGATES — THE SOIL BLOCK PARTIES

Not sure what we mean by aggregate? Think of aggregates as block parties in the soil. The aggregate—the chunk of soil—is the neighbourhood. The roads between are paved with tentacle-like fungal "mycelia," and the soil neighbourhood chunks are kept together by community action—by the exuded material from all the resident bacteria.

Good soil has these aggregates and air spaces, leaving a passageway for movement of air and water.

Sweet and Sour: a Recipe For Thinking about Acidity

He said I remember my late Great Aunt Barb—an avid gardener herself—telling me that the water in my late Great Aunt Peg's town always made "rough" tea. She was thankful that her own water made a "smooth" tea. I relate this because water often bears the hallmarks of the bedrock through which it percolates.

Most soils contain pulverized rock. In the same way bedrock affects water (and tea), that pulverized rock affects the characteristics of your soil. One of the key characteristics is the acidity or alkalinity of the soil.

Soil scientists use the term pH. It's a measure used to describe soil acidity or alkalinity. It's a good one too if you're a market gardener or agronomist. In the home garden, in most cases, it's overkill to measure and know your pH.

Let's stick with our cooking theme for this chapter: acid is sour, alkaline is sweet. The sweetness or sourness of soil is very important to consider because it affects the growth of soil microbes and affects the availability of nutrients to our vegetable plants. When soil is extremely sweet or sour, it can "lock up" nutrients, making them unavailable for chemical and biological processes in the soil. This lock-up can cause plant disorders and make plants susceptible to diseases.

We'll say it another way: when the sweetness or sourness of soil is balanced, there are more nutrients available to plants, and growing conditions are generally more favourable.

Here's an example: soil that's too sour makes a lousy home for rhizobium bacteria. They don't like it. We care about these little rhizobium bacteria because they attach to the roots of peas and their relatives, and "fix" nitrogen (capture nitrogen and fertilize the plant).

Soil that is too sweet may cause some elements to be unavailable to plants. The elements are there…but they're handcuffed to the soil.

At this point, any soil-studying gardener could rightly accuse us of simplifying soil pH. It's true that there are other factors

OBSERVING THE SOIL AROUND YOU

The next time you pass a construction site or cutaway on the side of a rural road or creek, you'll likely see a darker layer of soil near the surface. That's the thin ribbon of topsoil, the good stuff, on top. Underneath you'll see sub soils with less organic matter, which are usually less conducive to plant growth.

involved, such as the amount of rainfall, the use of certain types of fertilizer, and, in the case of urban gardens, whether the topsoil has been removed and replaced.

What's some no-guff advice on sweet and sour for you? Lime is suggested in many garden books as a cure for sour (acidic) soils; and sulphur for sweet (alkaline) soils. We believe that unless the soil is severely out of whack, adding organic matter—and all the microbes that come with it—is more practical. Sweet? Add organic matter. Sour? Add organic matter. Not sure? Add organic matter.

RECIPE FOR SOIL ABUSE

A garden should do well in the first few years after sod is removed and the garden planted. This is because soil has been humming with activity under sod, building organic matter levels as grass roots decay. A good supply of nutrients, plenty of organic matter, and soft soil are the starting point after sod is removed.

Then comes the crash and burn scenario: organic matter runs low, clay starts to compact, weeds start to grow. By year three the soil is cracking and hard. Beginners may benefit from first-year bliss, but over time the way to excellent gardens year after year is soil building.

1.

Soil Amendments

Compost

One of the easiest ways for home gardeners to boost the organic component of soil is through composting. The addition of compost opens up heavy clay soils to allow movement of air and water, yet also helps retain water in sandy soils.

The good news is that organic matter such as leaves, garden waste, and vegetable scraps become soil-building compost with very little effort. There are whole books written on this subject, and many municipalities have a compost hotline and demonstration area.

Most people have household and garden waste to recycle into garden soil. We can broadly group such organic (meaning it contains carbon) waste into four categories:

1. Coarse landscape waste such as branches from pruning trees and shrubs and stems and stalks from the garden. This coarse material can be a challenge to deal with because it breaks down more slowly than other waste. If you're really keen, you can rent a chipper-shredder annually. But the lowest input method of composting it is to chop up most of this into one-inch pieces and add it to your outdoor compost. It will compost eventually—we promise.

2. Grass Clippings. Nothing fires up a compost pile like grass clippings, although many people leave clippings on the lawn.

3. Fine kitchen waste: These are the slimy potato peels, coffee grounds, and crushed eggshells. They are very high in nitrogen and fire up the compost quickly.

4. Fine landscape waste includes leaves from trees as well as clippings from the vegetable and ornamental garden.

He said Consider a separate pile for slowly decomposing coarse waste if you have the space.

Forget the fancy, rotating composters that promise compost in a matter of days. Why complicate something that will take care of itself?

GREENS AND BROWNS

Like "meat and potatoes" served for dinner, "greens and browns" feed compost. The "greens" so often referred to in compost are the "meat." They add the protein or nitrogen to feed the microbes. The "browns" in compost are the potatoes. They add the fibre and carbon.

The compost diet needs both proteins and fibre. Some common greens for the compost include lawn grass, coffee grounds, hay, and vegetable peelings. Some of the browns include leaves, chopped corn stalks, straw, and newspaper.

Remember: we don't literally add meat—just high-protein or nitrogen-containing greens.

2.

3.

4.

She said Some fancy rotating composters are ideal for women because they are easy to turn. The "pile" method is just too heavy for most women to turn—and the stationary black compost units are too slow. They fill up quickly and additional units need to be added. Soon the whole yard is filled with compost barrels and the gardener is looking for a place to put the next leaf.

Compost Activators

I laugh whenever I walk past commercial compost-activator powders at garden centres. It's like buying vitamin C when you have a plate full of vitamin-rich fruit and vegetables in front of you. If you layer good garden soil with the contents of your composter, the soil will provide all the microbes required for great compost.

She said The trouble is that gardeners who have poor, depleted soils-soils that have been heavily fertilized or have lost some biological activity-might not have the microbe muscle they need to supercharge the compost. If possible, go to a great gardener and ask for a bit of their soil to inoculate your own compost when getting started!

Chemical herbicides can do damage to vegetable crops at low levels not detected by standard laboratory tests. I advise that purchased compost and soil be subject to an easy test (bioassay) that every gardener can do at home.

Cress Test Bioassay

Poorly made compost or contaminated soil can cause plants to fail. Try a home test using cress seeds (also sold as peppercress).

Start with two clean pots.

❀ Fill the first with a trusted commercial soil mix (this is called a "control").

❀ Fill the second with the compost or soil to be tested.

❀ Place 10 cress seeds on the surface of each pot, water gently, and set pots in a warm place.

❀ Seeds usually germinate within a couple of days.

HOME TESTS FOR SOIL AND AMENDMENTS

Because the standards and quality of soil, manure, and compost vary by producer, it's buyer beware when shopping for soil or compost.

Home Bioassay for Herbicides

The next level of testing is for herbicides. Susceptible crops include tomato, sunflowers, peas, and beans. Take one or more of these seeds and plant into a compost or soil that has passed the cress test above. By the time

Composting with worms is called vermicomposting.

the true leaves grow, you will know whether there is a problem with your compost or soil. Leaves will be narrow or weird compared to the leaves in the commercial potting mix. If there is anything other than normal growth, don't use the soil or compost for your vegetable garden.

She said Once when giving a talk in Alberta, I met a farm wife who composted cow manure for her garden. The cows were fed hay harvested from the road allowance-where the municipality had applied a herbicide. While it didn't seem to bug the cows, the manure killed most of the vegetable garden.

POT 1: TRUSTED SOIL MIX Expected results:	POT 2: MIX BEING TESTED May see:	POT 2: Results mean...
Most seeds come up overnight or within a few days.	Few seeds come up overnight, others appear slowly.	Compost or soil has slowed germination.
Seed roots grow down into soil.	Seed roots turn up away from soil.	Compost or soil has high salts.
After ten days seedlings look fine.	After ten days seedlings do not look healthy—they are falling over or in poor shape.	Compost or soil was not good or ready to use

I have never done a home bioassay. If my crops grow well, I won't seek out a potential problem.

Steve's young. Once he's lost his first crop to herbicides hidden in compost or manure he'll be more cautious.

Compost: Use Free Leaves

Never begrudge raking leaves again. Leaves are a gift. They're free, they're often abundant, and they make great compost, called leaf mould. If you don't have enough leaves, chances are that you have neighbours who do. If you can't fit them all into the composter, set them aside in bags or piles until spring. The saved leaves can then be mixed with garden and kitchen waste to balance the "greens" and "browns" added to the compost.

I am a regular at the city-sponsored leaf drop-off piles. The difference is I am there to pick up, not to drop off, leaves in the fall.

Leaves to avoid: Oak leaves are very slow to decompose. Either don't compost them, or chop them up before composting. Walnut leaves give off a toxin—called juglone—that inhibits the growth of some plants (see page 42), so don't add them to the compost pile.

Keep composting simple: layer leaves and soil, aerate the pile, cover it with soil, and then grow vegetables on it. With free leaf compost, you can turn a heavy clay soil into a rich, crumbly soil.

My compost was never finished quickly enough and I always had more than I could deal with. I bought a turning composter. It promised a fast return but was not as quick as I hoped. That changed this past summer, when I added leaves and worms to my turning composter. The whole thing changed magically—producing half a bucket of finished compost each week all summer. In the winter, my composter is frozen solid and can't accommodate any more kitchen stuff, so I use a worm bin to take care of the winter kitchen compost.

My Vancouver Island garden is in a climate where all the rats and racoons move to spend their retirement. This is another reason why I like the rat-proof rotating composter where I can process kitchen waste including my Bokashi system output.

A piece of mesh tied on one side makes a basic leaf composter.

LEAF COMPOSTING

Steve grows squash on top of his leaf composter all summer, giving him some added growing space.

Autumn: Leaves go into the composter, a couple of feet at a time layered with a couple of inches of soil.

Spring: Topped with soil and a crop planted.

Summer: Throughout the summer, use an old broomstick to aerate the pile, helping the leaves decompose more quickly. Push the broomstick all the way to the bottom of the pile, creating a vertical air channel.

Autumn again: Dig this compost into the vegetable garden and start again.

composting systems comparison

	steve	donna
Closed Plastic Composter	**YES** ❁ For fruit and veg scraps from the kitchen. ❁ Never turned. ❁ Instead, aerated with a broomstick.	**YES** ❁ For fine landscape materials and weeds. ❁ Takes at least a year. ❁ Never turned. Does not get hot enough to kill weed seeds or disease. ❁ After a year or so I spread it on shrub beds or garden.
Open Air Compost Pile	**YES** ❁ For yard waste.	**YES** ❁ On occasion Donna makes a hot compost pile to use up extra yard waste materials. This is not contained—just layered and turned. ❁ The heat kills weed seeds and bad bacteria.
Rotating Composter	**No** ❁ Please...what a waste of money.	**YES** ❁ Takes all the green kitchen waste that might otherwise attract rats because it is rodent-proof. ❁ Takes some leaves to get a good green-brown balance. ❁ Does not get hot enough to kill weed seeds or disease.
Worm Bin (see page 31)	**YES** ❁ Kitchen scraps, along with paper towels and shredded paper. ❁ So far, it doesn't take a huge volume of material.	**YES** ❁ Kitchen scraps, along with paper towels and tissue. ❁ All winter kitchen scraps go here, as the outdoor composter is frozen. ❁ In summer, they get just enough green and brown material to keep them alive. Some worms are added to rotating bin in summer. ❁ Worms do not kill seeds of veggies.
Bokashi*	**No** ❁ Donna gifted me a Bokashi, which I tried because the concept is neat. ❁ I stopped—too many compost systems...	**YES** ❁ Meat bits, bacon fat, bones and leftovers and anything not permitted in normal compost. ❁ Many municipalities now have pick-up of this kind of waste, but I keep all my own waste in-house by using a Bokashi.*
Overflow...	**YES** ❁ Extra leaves can go in a pile behind the shed or some bushes. ❁ This is the same as my open-air pile.	**YES** ❁ Extra leaves saved in garbage bags for composting later or mulching around shrubs. ❁ Leaves are also piled in an open mesh-enclosed bin with layers of finished compost.

*Bokashi is a sealed (anaerobic, or without air) system that digests kitchen wastes, including meat and dairy products. The waste goes into a sealed bin, and is inoculated with microorganisms. "Finished" material coming from a Bokashi system is then either buried in the garden or added to a composter. So think of Bokashi as a pre-composting system. Bokashi is not fed to worms.

Compost: Directly In The Garden

Instead of making a pile, some gardeners spread the goods out on their garden beds. This is called sheet composting, and it is a buffet spread for rats and other vermin.

She said I don't know about other people's dogs but mine would consider sheet composting an open invitation to trouble. I can just imagine my dog Kepla all sweet and innocent as she comes to the back door with potato skins and rotting melons on her fur after a back-rubbing roll in the compost.

Sheet composting works because there is plenty of time for the thin layer of compost materials to break down over the winter—but where it fails is that the compost never gets hot enough to kill weed seeds or diseases, as happens in a well-managed pile. The material should also be lightly tilled into the soil a few weeks before spring planting.

She said Garbage dogs eat everything-including compost-finished or not. This could-and has-resulted in dogs foaming at the mouth, shaking, and visiting the vet, with a $3000 bill to show for it. Keep dogs away from compost!

Visit www.GardenCoachesChat.com to read more about compost-induced doggie disorders.

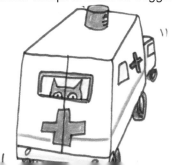

Compost: Kitchen Waste And Vermicomposting

If you haven't the space or inclination to use an outdoor composter, it's possible to compost indoors with the help of worms. It's called vermicomposting. The worms reside in a container the size of a recycling bin, and eat kitchen scraps. They eat and excrete, changing the scraps into worm castings, an excellent soil amendment.

Fruit scraps often come with fruit flies, which multiply quicker than lab rats on estrogen. People try to control fruit flies by freezing scraps before adding them to the worm bin—but if you forget once, it is game over, and flies in the wine to show for it. Donna uses predatory nematodes—purchased from commercial horticultural supply companies—in the worm bin at the first sight of flies. Nematodes enter the worm-like fruit fly larvae and, once inside, bacteria from the nematode kill the larvae. There's no harm to earthworms.

Visit www.GardenCoachesChat.com to read about Steve's kids' adventures in vermicomposting.

She said I'm too lazy-or is it smarter with age-to vermicompost in a recycling bin, so I use a tiered worm bin with a huge capacity for kitchen scraps. An added bonus is that it doesn't involve too much worm wrangling. A tap allows me to remove excess liquid that I can use to water plants.

After a worm compost test last year showed the beneficial bacteria counts were through the roof but

the beneficial fungus were low, I started adding more shredded office paper and leaves to the bin to increase fungal activity. Compost coming out of all worm bins is very high in good bacteria and low in bad bacteria.

He said My worm composter is in the basement, where a few fruit flies won't bother anyone.

Caution: Uncomposted Compost

While compost is an invaluable soil amendment that improves soil structure and adds nutrients to the soil…beware. Compost that is not fully decomposed can temporarily tie up soil nutrients—and this can stunt your plants. Poor compost may also contain alcohol…a result of too little air. Too bad young plants don't just get tipsy—but more likely they become stunted and die.

Animal Manure

Most livestock manure can be composted to give a nutrient-rich boost of organic matter to the garden. Don't add fresh manure to the garden, though, as it must first be composted. There are two reasons:

horse apples

❀ Before composting the manure can be "hot" and burn the crop. The products that "burn" are usually soluble salts.

❀ Properly aerated composting allows time for the microbial balance of the manure to shift from one with harmful micro-organisms to one with mainly beneficial ones.

cow pie

Contorted leaves might indicate herbicide residue in soil or compost.

When added to a compost pile, manure lights the fire, adding nitrogen that fires up microbes and gets the pile heating up. Manure can also inoculate a pile with a variety of new microbes. Horse manure is richer in nitrogen than cattle or swine manure.

She said

We visited one grower whose land had been regularly enriched with overly generous amounts of hog manure before he acquired it. The result? A soil rich in many elements-yet deficient too, thanks to one excess element bumping others off the soil particles. The moral? It's always possible to have too much of a good thing.

pig poop

Green Manures

A green manure is a crop that is grown to be dug into the soil before it is mature, adding organic matter. Examples are fast-growing crops such as fall rye, peas, clovers, and buckwheat. Roots grow down into the soil—improving it to a depth beyond that which cultivation would.

Want to make less work for yourself? Plant something that will die over the winter, so you don't need to hasten its demise in the spring with digging. Peas, buckwheat, and oats are good options.

Peat Moss

Peat moss is a made-in-North-America soil amendment, which, like compost, greatly improves the properties of soil.

While we think it's fine stuff for starting seeds and growing in containers, when it comes to amending the soil in the garden, we consider it an eco-extravagance. That's because most gardeners have kitchen or yard organics that could be composted. By all means, when dumping out old pots with peat-based soils, add this to the soil or compost. But think twice before buying it specifically as a soil additive. After all, it's basically mined carbon that we're adding to the garden—and eventually, to the atmosphere.

Mulches

Mulching is a technique where the soil surface is covered to decrease evaporation. It also stabilizes soil temperature. Along with modifying temperature and evaporation, mulching does one other very important thing: it inhibits weed growth.

There are countless materials that can be used for mulching. We'll discuss just a few below.

Straw and Hay Mulches

Straw and hay are two common mulching materials that come from farms. Straw is a bit more common as a mulch—and hay is sometimes used as a fertilizing material—but both can be used as mulches.

If you haven't been exposed to much agriculture, you might have only a foggy notion of the difference between hay and straw. Let's clear up the difference now, as it affects how you use them in the vegetable garden.

❋ Hay is grown as animal food. It is simply crops that are harvested green and then dried. It can be made from grasses, but often includes a "legume" such as alfalfa. Because it was harvested green, it contains more nitrogen, which is why some people use it as a fertilizer.

❋ Straw is the stalks left over once a crop such as wheat, oat, barley, or flax has been harvested. By the time it is bundled up, the stalks have dried down and don't contain the nitrogen they did at an earlier stage in the life cycle of the plant.

You might hear the term "clean" used to refer to hay and straw without a lot of seeds in them.

Soil-building fall rye is turned under when it is 10–15 cm (4–6 inches) tall.

Not only do I like to use straw for my strawberry bed, I like to use it on vegetable garden pathways. It sops up excess water, and keeps shoes from getting too muddy.

Bark and straw mulch on paths to suppress weeds and cover mud.

LAB TESTS FOR HERBICIDE CONTAMINATION

Many commercial soil-testing labs test for herbicides in soils and composts. You need to know what herbicide or group of products you think you are having a problem with or the cost will be prohibitive. Once you think you have pinpointed a herbicide group (a family of related products), the lab will charge five hundred to thousands of dollars to scan for those specific herbicides. Many herbicides have a half-life measured in weeks. Others take several years to break down and will not break down in the composting process. Don't forget: the easiest and least expensive way to test for contamination is a home bioassay (explained on page 28).

She said Using straw is like broadcasting weed seeds in the garden alongside your vegetables. Yes, straw breaks down and holds moisture, but what is this—a make-work camp? Let's face it, except for flax straw (which never seems to break down), the other straws—wheat, barley, and oats—all have a lot of seed. I use hay on my garlic and asparagus in the fall, and it usually breaks down by spring.

He said If the odd wheat or barley plant pokes up from my straw mulch, that's fine. I get fewer weeds than if I didn't mulch—and wheat or barley plants are hardly aggressive weeds. Hay, depending on when it's harvested, can have far more seeds than straw.

Wood Chips and Bark Chip Mulches

Because most vegetables are annuals, and intensive vegetable gardening often involves more than one crop per year in the same spot, there is no point using bark and wood chips in vegetable gardens (although they can be useful between rows of raised beds). They don't break down quickly enough.

One other point to consider is that as wood chips break down, microbes can pull nitrogen from the soil and starve plants. (Although this is short-term, and the nitrogen is returned once the mulch has decomposed.)

She said Instead of weeds between raised beds, I installed flattened cardboard and topped that with coarse wood chips. The chips between the beds will eventually break down. Wood is an organic material and won't become a make-work problem over time. My husband wondered why I didn't want to use landscape fabric under the wood. It's a problem, I explained, when one product (the wood) breaks down while the other product (the fabric) endures for a long time. When the wood in my current set-up breaks down, the cardboard will be gone too.

Plastic, Rubber Crumb, and Other Inert Mulches

There is a big difference between mulches made of organic materials and mulches made of inert materials such as crumb rubber or gravel.

If it won't break down naturally—and if you reconfigure your garden—then you'll have to remove the mulch. That's not worth the time in our minds.

She said Inert materials never really add to a garden and they start to get a layer of dead plant material and dust on them, which, over time, becomes soil. Believe me—if you think it is hard to weed in soil, just imagine how hard it is to weed between gravel and plastic. Impossible! The weed roots love the growing zone beneath the plastic and they spread out wide and far, making them impossible to pull.

Soil and Compost Guff Busted

Guff Says

Those humble tubers—potatoes—build soil.

GUFFAWERS RESPOND

The potato theory goes something like this: when new gardeners move in, they should plant the whole yard in potatoes.

Donna's husband Keith remembers his grandparents planting potatoes for soil-building at their new home in the late 1940s. Donna heard the same rumblings but ignored them when she planted her first garden in the early 1980s.

Guff pushers say the soil will benefit in some way from big-scale potato planting. Truth is, potatoes are heavy feeders: commercial potato producers use crop rotations to avoid depleting soils. In other words, this old wives' tale probably started because new or "virgin" soils could support a potato crop at least once.

Guff Says

Blend kitchen waste and pour it on the garden.

GUFFAWERS RESPOND

It seems daft to us: It makes a mess (imagine cleaning the blender every day), and it packs the materials down finely so they mat rather than compost. Where, for instance, would we pour this slurry in the winter when the ground is frozen? Imagine the festering puddles in the spring? Would they just feed noxious microbes waiting for a carbohydrate source? Part of composting is the benefit of reusing the fibre…so why blend it?

Garden Soils:

My soil is as hard as cement, and it has formed cracks. What should I do?

Sounds like all your organic matter is gone and all that is left is the inorganic or mineral parts of the soil. **She said** Clay, which can become hard like cement when dry, is actually good, but it desperately needs organic matter and active microbes to function properly.

Amend the soil with lots of biologically active organic matter in the spring or fall, when it's not too hard to dig, or simply top-dress the garden all season long with compost. Avoid digging or turning soil for at least a season. Gardening and soil building is like the Slow Food movement. It takes a while to prepare a really good soil and there is no rushing it!

34

Soil lacking organic matter cracks when dry.

Some people say that I shouldn't dig the soil—it's not the most natural practice. Is this true?

He said There's probably a microbe-rights or worm-rights group waiting to pounce on me for saying this...but seriously, if you want "natural" soil, go live in the woods and don't garden.

Some people believe that digging the soil creates unnecessary work and harms populations of worms and beneficial microbes. In a no-dig system, worms are employed to move the organic matter that is placed over top of beds.

I believe that digging, within reason, is important. It's an opportunity to work in organic matter such as compost and green manures, and provides crops a loose, well-aerated soil—which is especially important for root crops such as carrots and parsnips.

She said I'm against deep digging. I think that reduced digging will be the wave of the future, but it is also the wave of the past. Forests and grasslands are never turned except on the small microscopic worm and microbe level, and natural soils have more organic matter than most worked topsoil today.

Reduced digging does not rule out adding compost and turning it lightly and shallowly into the surface (two to four inches at the most), but the soil-destroying era of double and tripling digging is ancient history.

Can I use municipal compost for on my vegetable garden?

She said Some municipal compost has killer levels of salts.

In general, municipal composts are not ideal for growing vegetables because it is hard for a municipality to control what people dump in their "compost." The final product will contain whatever contaminants were in the initial contributions.

Steve adds: Here in Toronto I have found glass shards in the municipal compost, so I don't use it.

Real Gardeners Don't...

Real vegetable gardeners don't treat soil like dirt.

Have a bit of an intimate relationship with your soil: Pick it up, squeeze it, smell it. OK, we're not recommending you think of it at night...but it's a good sign if you do.

He said Talking about treating soil like dirt... I once worked at a nursery with a beautiful soil. It was adjacent to a marsh and the soil was rich and black. But the rototiller was run down those rows so often that the soil was pulverized to death: the structure was removed, and the constant exposure of the organic matter to air sped up its breakdown.

Summary: Soils—Food for a Good Harvest

All soil textures can be improved by the addition of organic matter. One common trait of "working" vegetable garden soils is that they will become depleted of organic matter over time. This doesn't mean you need to change your soil. Simply build upon what you have by making or buying compost and other organic matter. Make it an ongoing process, and do it annually.

Both Steve and Donna make composting a big part of what they do. If you are barely getting by in the garden and don't have time to make compost, buy some. In the same way yogurt puts good microbes into our digestive tract, good compost builds the soil with microbes.

Donna and Steve's Thumbs-Up Guide

GUFF & GARDENING STUFF		DONNA	STEVE
1. Climate	Row Covers	Up	Down
	Cold Frames	Up	Up
2. Soil	Rotating Composters	Up	Down
	Rototilling	Down	Up

Garden Coaches Chat: No guff. Lots of fun. *for more details visit www.GardenCoachesChat.com*

35

WHAT'S RIGHT?

There is no "right" way to plan your garden. Instead of focusing on what's right, think about what suits your needs.

PLANNING A VEGETABLE GARDEN

While commercial market gardening necessitates the use of straight rows and uniformity, the home gardener is free from those constraints and can create a garden of any size, shape, or pattern.

Maybe your garden has the symmetrical layout of a commercial market garden, or the creative flair of an abstract painting. Both are fine.

He said

My Dad, Bob, grew up in a household that valued straight lines. For him, all those straight lines were begging to be curved—so his garden beds are flowing and rounded, with not a straight edge to be found. Dad instilled in me a love of rounded beds...though I like straight lines in my vegetable garden!

She said

My Dad, Harvey, was raised on rows. Straight rows. He did not tolerate curves or decorative vegetables and would not let my mother slip even a few ornamental vegetables in with the flowers. Luckily my dad was too busy farming to see what my mom was actually doing in the vegetable garden.

Top 3 Sensible Planning Tips

1. Don't be afraid to change your plan and squeeze in new crops.

2. Don't hide the vegetable garden—show it off.

3. Take advantage of any spot at all—even if it seems too small.

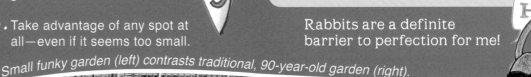

DETOX FOR PERFECTIONISTS

If you think you might be too much of a perfectionist, think of vegetable gardening as an antidote. It's detox for perfectionists.

The reason is simple: With gardening, you're never fully in control. Whether it's unexpected weather, a flock of birds, weed seeds from the neighbours, or a squirrel, there are always barriers to perfection.

That's fine. A well-tended but imperfect vegetable garden will still yield well for you.

He said

Rabbits are a definite barrier to perfection for me!

Small funky garden (left) contrasts traditional, 90-year-old garden (right).

	Formal	Informal	Bit of Both
The Look	Formal	Informal	Bit of Both
The Workload	Lots, I'm Keen	In Between	Minimal Work
The Harvest	Need Lots	Need Some	Enough for One
The Future	Will Expand	Might Expand	Won't Expand

Vegetable Garden Planning Exercise

There is no right way to organize your vegetable garden. If you think we're trying to avoid writing a chapter on planning, we're not. We want you to focus on your needs and wants.

Focusing on your needs and wants will guide you in the size and placement of your garden, based on the "look" and amount of work (and harvest) you want.

Here are examples of how you can apply your answers to the exercise when planning your garden:

The Look: If you're attracted to a formal appearance, you might want vegetables in blocks or rows in a dedicated bed, away from ornamentals. But if you prefer to keep things informal, you might go for a cottage-style garden and dot tomato plants amongst your flowers.

The Workload: We don't begrudge spending a lot of time in the garden: we write about gardening, so it's our job. But you might not have a lot of time. If that's the case, keep it small and avoid techniques that take a lot of time.

The Harvest: If you can use lots of fresh produce, then it makes sense to grow lots. If you're growing for one, you might decide to keep the garden small.

The Future: If you have plans to expand the garden in future years, consider leaving space to expand. Remember this when planting small trees that might grow larger and shade future expansion.

Planning Considerations

Now that you've thought about the look, workload, volume, and future growth of your vegetable garden, let's look at a few other planning considerations. Start with either form or with function—but ultimately strive to bring the two together.

Access Within the Garden

Kneel down and stretch out your arm and see how far you can reach while digging with a trowel. As you plan your garden, make sure you can reach all areas of the vegetable garden bed from the edge, a pathway, stepping stone, or a spot left empty for footsteps.

She said When kneeling I can barely dig a trowel into the middle of a bed that is four feet across, and I am pretty tall for a girl. Obviously shorter girls or guys will want even narrower beds.

Top garden is casual, while bottom garden has precisely measured rows.

If you keep beds to approximately 1 m (3.5 feet) wide you should be able to reach most parts of the bed without stepping onto it. Before making the bed, test the width to make sure it's comfortable for you: too wide and some simple digging might require a balancing act of standing tiptoe on one foot, with your trowel in one outstretched arm—and the other arm propping you up.

She said Stepping on soil ruins soil structure by squeezing out air spaces and compacting clay—so always plan ahead so you won't have to step on soil.

Blocks Versus Rows
Traditional rows allow access with a hoe to cultivate and control weeds. But that means a lot of unplanted ground, which can be a luxury in cramped home gardens. Planting in solid blocks or wide rows doesn't leave as much space for a hoe, but is a better use of limited space. Once established, dense plantings choke out many weeds.

Some gardeners prefer blocks of rows, with crops planted in a block along the length of each row, instead of several skinny single plant rows. Both Donna and Steve play around with this but—really—there is no right or wrong way.

He said I like to use blocks of one square metre (one square yard) for most veggie crops.
The exception is tomatoes, which I put in a long row that is two plants wide. When they're in blocks, the plants in the middle languish.

Precision
Don't get too caught up in precision! We think it's a waste of time. While seed catalogues specify exact planting depths and spacing, these are simply guidelines. Many crops can be planted by hand-scattering seeds and then covering with a thin layer of soil. Other seeds can be simply pressed into the soil.

From left: vegetables and ornamentals co-exist; nasturtium flowers add colour to the vegetable garden; traditional rows.

Shape
Not big on squares and rectangles? Then make rounded, scalloped, or variously shaped gardens. Let the shape of the available space be your guide or inspiration.

Sunlight
With few exceptions, veggies need sunlight—especially at midday—so don't hide your garden on the north side of the house, behind a fence, or under a big tree and hope for success.

Grow taller plants where they won't shade neighbouring smaller ones.

Planning for Appearance

There's no reason for a vegetable garden to be drab. There are many ways to enliven it. Here are a few ideas.

From bottom left: red and green beets in a block; a row of colourful Swiss chard.

Alternately, you might want to edge the vegetable garden with flowering herbs such as lavender or plants with variegated leaves.

He said
I like to plant a few gladiolus bulbs in the vegetable patch, something Shelley's grandmother taught me. I'm a big fan of colourful mixed Swiss chard, which has great ornamental value.

bed to give a consistent look. At a minimum, you can contour the edges of your vegetable garden to blend with ornamental gardens.

Planning the Unplanned

Unplanned crops arrive in the garden from seeds blowing in the wind, seeds dropped the previous season, and seeds in composted kitchen scraps.

And that's good news.

Vary Textures and Shapes

Select vegetables with a variety of leaf types to vary shapes and texture in the garden. This applies whether you have a dedicated vegetable patch or whether you're interplanting your vegetables with ornamentals in the flowerbed. Picture fernlike dill leaves poking up from behind large, ruffled lettuce leaves.

She said
I grow asparagus as much for its ferny texture and bright red berries in the fall as for the spears in spring.

Add Colour
Don't be afraid to add colour to your vegetable garden, whether flowers or coloured veggies.

She said
I love red lettuce. A recent favourite was Freckles, a red, speckled variety of romaine lettuce that I bought as soon as I saw it for sale at the market. Of course I have not been able to find it again!

Incorporate Landscape Themes
By themes we mean things such as fences and pathways—permanent fixtures in the garden.

Don't be afraid to incorporate themes found in the rest of your yard. For example, if flagstones are part of your ornamental garden, use them to create vegetable garden pathways or a border around the vegetable garden. If you have a deck, you might consider a wood-framed garden

Self-seeded lettuce makes great use of space in the vegetable garden. Like dandelion seeds, lettuce seeds grow attached to a silky parasol that allows them to float around on a summer breeze and nestle in garden nooks that you would never think to seed. So your lettuce will pop up amongst the tomatoes, peas, potatoes, and even in the asparagus patch. Where there is space, let them grow: where there is not, remove them. They will fill the holes in your garden for you.

Mix colours, shapes, and textures. From bottom left: pointy leaf lettuce; ruffled kale with poppies; lettuce starting to flower; mottled zucchini leaves; pointy green onions.

Big garden: every sunny spot in Donna's daughter Kalen's yard sprouts vegetables and fruits.

Vegetable Garden Size

Thought you had to crunch numbers to figure out how many plants you need for a given harvest? Forget it. No matter how much time you spend trying to predict yield, gardening—like farming—is unpredictable. If you're reading this book, you're probably looking for simple strategies. Try this one:

Think of yourself first:

❀ Consider how much time you want to spend.

Now think of the garden:

❀ Figure out how much of your yard you're willing to allocate to a vegetable garden.

❀ Use some stakes and twine to divide the garden into sections, by crop.

❀ Then plant those sections with your vegetables.

❀ Use the same approach when buying seeds.

He said Don't waste too much time calculating spacing. Just decide what you want to grow—then figure out how to squeeze it all into the vegetable garden. Maybe that even means adding a few veggie plants to the flower border.

My five-year-old daughter Emma sagely advised Donna and me to make certain we leave ample space for pumpkin plants after Emma's pumpkin plant ran amok in her patch and choked out everything else.

Putting It on Paper

When you make a plan, all you're doing is:

❀ Defining the garden area

❀ Listing the crops you want to grow

❀ Then slotting those crops into that space

You can do it on the computer, but all you really need is paper, a pencil, and a good eraser.

If you're worried that you don't have the artistic skills or gardening knowledge necessary to sketch out a rough garden plan, stop worrying. I can barely draw a stick person—but I can make a garden plan. You can too. **He said**

She said I like to use large sheets of graph paper for planning. Each square is one quarter inch across. I use the scale of one square equals one square foot in the garden. Most average front or backyards can be drawn on one sheet of paper. I put in the permanent fixtures such as fences, paved areas and, of course, the house or apartment and large permanent trees. Mark north and south on the plan and then look for areas that get the most light. These are your future vegetable garden areas.

Small garden: a framed box in a community garden is packed and bountiful.

From left: herbs thyme, sage and parsley can be planted close to the kitchen.

She said I called in a plumber to add a tap on the back of my older house because that is where the plants are!

Think of the Kitchen

Unless you live in a warm climate, the vegetable garden is unlikely to be active year round. But the enthusiast can dig parsnips from under the snow, get an early start with a hotbed, and continue to harvest hardy crops such as kale and Brussels sprouts late into the fall.

Why do we mention this?

So you'll think about how close your vegetable garden—or parts of it—should be to your kitchen.

He said I keep a large patch of parsley near the back door so that in muddy and snowy weather, it's nearby and picking it doesn't entail tromping through lots of mud.

He said Some people wonder about the safety of rainwater collected on roofs. Water quality depends on a number of things including the roofing material, presence of bird droppings, raccoon feces—and the quality of the rainwater itself. I don't drink water from my rain barrel, nor do I wash vegetables in it. But I do water my garden with it. Sure, I could test it... but isn't that setting a double standard when I don't know anything about the quality of water used to produce food I buy at the store?

Steve's daughter, Emma, fills her watering can right in the garden.

Where's the Water Source?

This is a biggie. Put the garden near a tap or rain barrel—or get a hose long enough to reach your garden.

Not a lot of water but lots of land? Some farmers leave land fallow in dry areas to conserve water in the soil for the next year.

Tap nearby? Plan for a water source near the garden.

Check for Sunlight

Without moving buildings or felling trees, you're probably stuck with the light conditions that exist in your garden. The thing to remember is that most vegetables do best in full sunlight. Ideally, that means at least six hours of sunlight every day but there are exceptions, and you can try locations with partial sunlight.

If you don't have perfect light, try anyway: you're not a market gardener trying to get perfect crops.

No veggiephobia here: Maggi's front vegetable garden in spring and summer.

SHADES OF GREY: VEG FOR PARTIAL SUN

Is your vegetable garden in deep shade? If so, stop reading—we can't help. But if you have partial shade (that, of course, means partial sun) then you can grow vegetables.

Below we've listed crops that are worth trying in a part-shade situation. There are others, but start with these. In general, leafy crops are a good bet in the shade.

arugula, asparagus, beans, beets, broccoli, cucumbers, kale, kohlrabi, lettuce, parsley, peas, potato, radish, sorrel, spinach, squash, turnip

Consider Nearby Trees

There is a myth that tree roots only grow out as far as the edge of the tree canopy. If you plant a garden and start watering it you will quickly find out just how far tree roots grow. Willow tree roots will gallop right over to a garden with enriched soil and ample water. Evergreens will also move in quickly. Expect roots well beyond the drip line of a tree—and plan for it by raising the garden beds, if necessary.

Some members of the walnut family give off a compound called juglone. While some vegetables don't take notice of juglone, others, such as asparagus, cabbage, eggplant, pepper, and tomato hate it and will die or have stunted growth. If you can't move your garden away from a walnut tree, raised beds, which give good drainage, help to minimize the effect.

See www.GardenCoachesChat.com for information about juglone-sensitive vegetable crops.

He said We bought our current house in the spring, before the trees were in leaf, so I didn't notice that my neighbour, Troy, has a massive black walnut tree in his backyard. The tree towers over one side of my yard too. Only after I had bought the house did I find out that the previous owner had given up on veggies because of that tree. In a state of despair, I raised the soil level and tried a veggie garden anyway, and, to date, am getting good crops.

She said In the summer of 2010 my garden at Qualicum Beach was on its own. Yes, we have an irrigation system but I couldn't get out to see if it was set correctly and when I showed up in late July, many things had perished or gone to seed prematurely because of drought stress. The remarkable exception was the yellow, green, and

Vegetables as ornamentals. From left: fennel flowers; snazzy veggie pots; zucchini in bloom; dill and beets together for textural contrast.

purple beans planted under the partial shade of a 40-year-old catalpa tree. When I arrived on site they were not only thriving, the super crop of beans was ready to eat. It was almost as if the plants were saying, "Welcome." It proved to me that shade can be our friend during an exceptionally hot dry spell.

The Yard

Out Front

As the story goes, when Steve's parents bought their home, the neighbour was worried that they might be vegetable gardeners who would plant tomatoes in the front yard... where everyone could see them.

Today, all these years later, there is some veggiephobia out there, especially in suburban areas. We're not talking

SALTY SOIL IN YOUR FRONT YARD?

If you've been overly generous with the road salt over the winter—or your municipality has—it is possible to have soil salt levels that damage plants.

We're not trying to sound alarmist here. Steve gardened in the front yard of a house on a busy street—where frequently passing snowplows spread ample salt—and never had a problem. But it is possible.

Simply put, one of the main reasons too much salt in the soil is a problem is that it makes water unavailable to plants. Plants can be stunted, or they can die. So what should you do if you suspect high salt levels?

Stop fertilizing. That means both organic and inorganic fertilizers. Fertilizers by nature contain lots of nutrients—and those nutrients often occur in a salt form.

Try flood irrigation, making sure drainage is good enough to allow the extra water to escape. The water will wash away the salt.

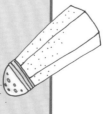

about obscene images here: we're talking about growing vegetables. And as we said earlier, there is lots you can do to make the vegetable garden look nice. Be creative and your front-yard veggie garden could look nicer than neighbouring homes with cookie-cutter shrubs and lawn.

He said I recently met a gardener who transformed his front yard into a vegetable garden—even planting the boulevard between the road and the sidewalk with vegetables.

She said If I planted my boulevard I would be afraid of peeing dogs and browsing bunnies.

Here in Toronto you have to be afraid of bureaucrats who'll tell you it's illegal to grow veg on your boulevard.

43

Out Back: Backyards, Alleys, and Laneways

Many people encroach a bit on city property by planting in a back alley. If this is your sunniest spot, go for it. Remember it is also a place people walk their dogs and dust from cars lands on food—so be sure to install signs and beg dog walkers to avoid letting their dogs pee on your little space and wash everything before eating it.

Consider vining or staking plants—at least the edible parts will be above the average pee-line of a male dog.

A DEDICATED BED?

Maybe you don't want a dedicated garden for edibles. That's fine. As long as you give edibles the light, water, and space they require, it's perfectly fine to interplant them with ornamental plants.

Consider colour when planning: blue-fleshed potatoes have pretty blue flowers.

Vegetable Garden Planning

Will air pollution and dust from cars make my vegetables unsafe to eat?

He said Is there air pollution and dust wherever the veggies you buy at the supermarket are grown? Of course. Enough said.

What about lead in the soil?

Thanks to a longstanding lead addiction in our society, garden soils—especially urban ones—probably have more lead than was originally there. The past use of two products plays a big role in soil lead levels:

* Leaded gasoline
* Lead-based paint

Urban areas have more buildings and fences on which offending paints were used—and urban areas, naturally, have more roads and cars, so were more often cloaked in lead-laced exhaust.

Sources vary when it comes to pinpointing a soil lead measurement that is cause for alarm. The Ontario Ministry of the Environment says there is minimal risk in consuming homegrown vegetables grown in soil containing less than 200 parts per million (ppm) of lead, and not to eat vegetables grown in gardens with soil lead levels above 1000 ppm. The University of Minnesota says that up to 300 ppm of lead is acceptable, unless there are kids around. That's because kids play outdoors and are more likely to get soil in their mouths—intentionally or not. If there are kids around, it advises, 100 ppm is acceptable.

Brace yourself: There's no simple answer when it comes to acceptable lead levels. That is because the availability of lead and other contaminants to plants will vary with soil type. Then, to complicate things, some plants take up more lead than others.

Here's a no-guff way to approach lead: If you suspect your soil has a high lead level (and even if you don't) wash your produce, as soil and dust on the produce probably have more lead than the produce itself. If you're in an older part of town, garden away from buildings where paint may have flaked off. If you've reason to be suspicious of unusually high soil lead levels, test the soil, rather than fretting every time you eat something from the garden.

She said If you live in an older home on a busy street like I do, you can test your garden soil for lead. Contact the government body responsible for the environment or agriculture, and enquire about laboratories accredited to test for soil contaminants.

She said Most lipsticks have more lead in them than garden soils. Pick your battles.

Keep shading to a minimum with well planned rows and blocks.

Planning Guff Busted

Guff Says
Grow in rows that are aligned north-south so crops don't shade each other.

GUFFAWERS RESPOND

We talked about this myth a lot. Because neither of us is a firm adherent to it, we started looking at gardens and farms to see what other people do.

Our suggestion? This is guff. You're better to spend your time thinking about the placement of tall plants where they will not shade shorter plants. Whether rows run north-south or east-west is of little consequence.

Guff Says
You need a plan that says where to plant your crops and how to space them.

GUFFAWERS RESPOND

He said

Planning is great, but sometimes it's best to just dig in. I had a client who really wanted a vegetable garden, but was afraid to dig in until she had it perfectly planned. Why wait? I'm like a bull in a china shop when it comes to the garden—I need to just grab a spade and get to work.

That's what I did with my stone-walled herb garden this year. I had a sense of what I wanted, so did not plan in advance.

She said Although I draw plans for other people, I hate to commit to a plan in my own garden. When my husband Keith refused to help with a proposed backyard feature until I showed him a plan, I sketched up a bird's-eye view on a napkin at a restaurant-then he agreed to the project on the spot and got to work enthusiastically. Gardeners having trouble coming up with a plan, combined with partners who won't get to work until they see a plan, can hire a professional if they don't feel confident.

Real Vegetable Gardeners Don't...

Real vegetable gardeners don't worry about what people will say about their garden plan.

They grow what they want, where they want, and how they want.

Real vegetable gardeners don't worry what the neighbours will say about where they plant their vegetables.

The whole property is fair game.

Summary: Planning a Vegetable Garden

There is more than one type of vegetable garden and more than one type of gardener. A little forethought can maximize success, but planning can be overrated too. Ease into it and let it evolve. A garden, like any hobby, expands to fit the time and space available.

Visit www.GardenCoachesChat.com to see sample garden plans.

Donna and Steve's Thumbs-Up Guide

GUFF & GARDENING STUFF		DONNA	STEVE
1. Climate	Row Covers	Up	Down
	Cold Frames	Up	Up
2. Soil	Rotating Composters	Up	Down
	Rototilling	Down	Up
3. Planning	Planning Perfectionism	Down	Down
	Flowers Mixed with Veg	Up	Up

Garden Coaches Chat: No guff. Lots of fun.
for more details visit www.GardenCoachesChat.com

45

Hmph

MAKING A VEGETABLE GARDEN

Top 3 Sensible Garden-Making Tips

1. Measure and mark the garden first.

2. Dig out turf with a flat spade or smother it prior to planting.

3. A garden does not need to be raised

Use the 3-4-5 rule to lay out a square corner.

5'
4'
3'
90°

Marking Where to Dig

Are you a Square Head?
If you really want right-angled corners in your garden, pull out the high-school math. You can use the Pythagorean Theorem.

She said I was never a math scholar, but one of my first jobs in horticulture at the University of Alberta involved laying out trial beds for new flowers and vegetables. "Simplé, said my boss, who proceeded to instruct me in the use of the 3-4-5 rule (Pythagorean Theorem) for making a garden bed!

$$a^2+b^2=c^2$$

He said You must be joking—the Pythagorean Theorem in the garden? I eyeball the corners and refuse to measure in my own garden.

Not-So-Square Beds
If you are planning curved beds, either dig these out free-form or lay down a garden hose to use as a guide.

Sodbusting

The first step to making your vegetable garden is sodbusting. There are no two ways about it: removing or smothering the lawn (or other vegetation) to make your vegetable garden takes a bit of work.

Smother It
Cover the lawn with a removable covering such as a tarp for four or more weeks, which kills the lawn by blocking sunlight. Alternately, cover it with a biodegradable covering such as newspaper or cardboard topped with layers of finished compost, lawn clippings, and leaves. Finish with a layer of garden soil on top of the organic materials. The effect of this layering is to smother the underlying grass—but unlike the tarp technique, this method also builds the soil.

As you've read, we believe that composting is the ticket to good garden soil. Making a new garden can be an opportunity for both

46

From left: smother a lawn instead of removing sod; a formal school garden; situate tall plants such as sunflowers where they won't shade neighbours.

composting and incorporating compost. If you decide to try the above approach, just skip the next section and never lift sod again!

She said My daughter Chelsie uses the soil-smothering approach to build garden beds and she finds it best to stick with shallow-rooted crops such as lettuce and cauliflower in the bed's first summer. What a great way to put extra compost and leaves to work. And to teach Mom a new lesson.

By Flathead Spade

If you're in a hurry for root vegetables—or simply enjoy digging—you'll have to apply a bit of brawn and use a spade, unless you plan to rent a gas-powered sod stripper to remove vegetation.

If you don't have a flathead spade, now is a good time to get one. Holding the spade upright, push it down with your foot so that it cuts into the lawn. Now use the spade to cut

an outline of your garden bed into the lawn. Then, within the area of the bed, make long cuts the width of the spade, so you have a series of parallel lines giving a series of rows of turf roughly the width of your spade.

Now comes the rewarding part: get the spade under the edge of one of these rows and hold it nearly horizontal, so that you can use it to chop at the roots of the grass. Leave as little soil on the turf as you practically can. When you get the knack of this, you'll be able to chop and roll back your turf like a roll of sod. Of course, the gas-powered sod stripper does this work in a matter of minutes, but it does make a huge noise, contributes to pollution, and has to be picked up and returned to the rental shop.

Keep the turf. Then pile it root-side up, and leave it to decompose for the season. It will turn into a pile of fertile soil that you can add back to your garden next year.

She said Some rental companies deliver heavy equipment, such as sod strippers, if you don't want to haul it home yourself, but Steve and I agree: gas-powered sod strippers make such a racket we prefer the quiet approach of a flat spade.

Working Newly Cleared Soil

Once you have removed all of the grass, use a garden spade or fork to cultivate the newly cleared soil, turning it 15–20 cm (6–8 inches) deep. As you dig, break up clumps. A fork is particularly useful on heavy clay ground that sticks together as it is turned.

A garden rake can be used once the ground is tilled to level it and rake out roots and twigs.

47

From left: a raised bed framed with lumber; Steve's unframed, raised beds

Types of Vegetable Garden Beds

An unframed, ground-level bed is fine in many situations.

Unframed Bed

In its simplest form, a garden bed is cut out of the turf, and the level of the garden soil is similar to that of the nearby ground, or slightly raised once amendments are added and soil is fluffed with a fork.

This simple form is perfectly fine in many cases and works especially well where the soil drains quickly.

He said When starting a new garden, many people think it's necessary to buy "good" soil. Buying new soil every time the soil gets hard is like buying a new car every time yours runs out of gas.

She said I get a charge out of the garden centre bags of "topsoil" which usually do not contain any topsoil, and are often soilless growing media and will not replace topsoil if you are trying to fill a new raised bed.

Basic Raised Bed

A raised bed provides improved drainage and, best of all, the soil warms up faster in the spring. It is especially useful where the soil is heavy or poorly drained,

Making a raised bed can entail bringing in additional soil, but doesn't have to. Copious amounts of compost and raking soil from the pathways onto the beds will achieve the same effect. Over time, with a continued addition of compost, the bed becomes higher.

Raised beds don't need sides to hold the soil in place. In fact, they're easier to dig without sides. The soil might migrate a bit over the summer, but not a lot. A height of 15–20 cm (6–8 inches) is easily achieved without side boards.

He said I grow onions along the sloped edges of my raised beds as a way to make use of that space.

Edged Raised Bed

A more formal look can be achieved by edging your raised beds with brick, stone, or wood. The beds can be as simple or as complicated as you wish.

She said I'm worried about chemicals in treated lumber, so avoid using it for raised beds. Instead, I use naturally resistant Douglas fir timber, plastic lumber, or bricks.

He said Wood Preservation Canada (which bills itself as a national association representing manufacturers of treated wood products) advises, "Do not use pressure-treated wood where it may become a component of food or animal feed. For example, treated wood should not be in direct contact with silage." I followed up about vegetable gardening and was told: "There are no restrictions against using pressure-treated wood to build containers. We have a few recommendations: Do not plant anything closer than 12 inches to the pressure-treated wood; and line your container with a breathable plastic liner." My take on the response? Stick with untreated wood for your edibles.

Garden-Making Guff Busted

Guff Says

A garden bed should be edged with lumber.

GUFFAWERS RESPOND

In our opinion, hauling lumber into the garden is the quickest way to make it ugly! Garden graveyard or what? Our suggestion is to freshen up the grassy edge of the bed with a flat spade every couple of years.

She said I wonder why so many community gardens are built around the principal of timber-framed raised beds? Some are even lined with synthetic fabric that takes forever to decompose. What a mess that will be in the long term when the boards have decomposed but the fabric is still there.

From left: raised beds can be edged with stones or bricks; soil raked into raised beds with plank walkways.

GARDEN RIP

49

Guff Says

Double- and triple-digging is good for the garden.

GUFFAWERS RESPOND

Where topsoil is shallow, this sort of digging frenzy can mix good soil with bad. Multiple digging also adds a lot of oxygen to the soil, which contributes to a faster breakdown of organic matter—and this is not a good thing.

Guff Says

Raised beds are the best choice.

GUFFAWERS RESPOND

Raised beds are not the best choice in all situations. In sandy soils, raised beds mean water becomes a limiting factor in the summer. But a raised bed alleviates wet, oxygen-starved roots where the soil is wet. Consider your soil type and drainage before building a raised bed.

Q & A: Garden Making

Q: Is a rototiller bad?

He said

A: Not in my opinion. This is a situation where the old adage of everything in moderation applies. I have one. But...I've seen beautiful soil wrecked by monthly rototilling. It can be physically demanding to wrestle a rototiller around the garden. And you will get a healthy dollop of exhaust fumes while you're at it. But if you have a large garden, a rototiller not only saves time—it works in compost well. It's one of the few worthwhile gadgets, Donna.

From left: avoid treated lumber; be creative with edging (note metal edging used here).

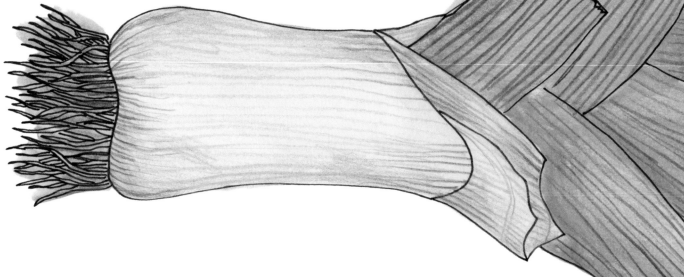

She said Rototillers are just one more noisemaker and polluter in the garden. I sold mine and declined my mother's when she tried to give it to me. If I had an acreage or if I decided to till my soil I might rethink this. I simply fluff the surface of the soil and just keep topping it up with organic matter. No heavy duty turning for this lightweight.

Real Vegetable Gardeners Don't...

Real vegetable gardeners don't discard the turf they have removed to make a new garden bed.

Instead, they pile it, soil side up, to break down into rich, friable topsoil.

He said OK, sorry for the garden jargon here. Friable means crumbly—and that's a good thing because soil that is friable usually has lots of organic matter such as compost (or decomposed turf) in it.

Real vegetable gardeners don't place landscape fabric under their raised beds.

This hampers the movement of worms and microbes in the soil below the raised bed from moving into the soil in the raised bed.

Summary: Building a Vegetable Garden

Removing or covering turf allows you to jump right in with garden making. There is no need to spend money at the hardware store for lumber or raised bed kits if you don't want to.

Donna and Steve's Thumbs-Up Guide

GUFF & GARDENING STUFF		DONNA	STEVE
1. Climate	Row Covers	Up	Down
	Cold Frames	Up	Up
2. Soil	Rotating Composters	Up	Down
	Rototilling	Down	Up
3. Planning	Planning Perfectionism	Down	Down
	Flowers Mixed with Veg	Up	Up
4. Garden Making	Pythagorean Theorem	Up	Down
	Double Digging	Down	Down

Garden Coaches Chat: No guff. Lots of fun.
for more details visit www.GardenCoachesChat.com

CROP SELECTION & ROTATION

5

Top 3 Sensible Selection Tips

1. Grow what you like.
2. Use volunteer crops to get an early start.
3. Shake it up baby—practise rotation (or don't).

What to Grow

There's no right or wrong when it comes to choosing crops to grow in your vegetable garden. That's why we won't tell you what to grow: It really depends on what you like.

So that's the first message: **grow what you like.**

If what you like is grown commercially in warmer climates, it doesn't mean you must automatically rule out growing it. Even in regions with less heat than is ideal for heat-loving crops such as watermelons and peppers, you're bound to find gardeners pushing the limits and finding ways to grow them.

I'm a fig fan, so I keep a few fig trees, even though they're not hardy here in Toronto. Where there's a will there's a way.

He said

He said The year I hauled in 20 pounds of parsnips to store, my wife Shelley made it clear that I shouldn't expect her to eat that many parsnips. Undeterred by my bumper crop, I decided to try a parsnip wine recipe. The result was revolting, even unsuited for use as cooking wine. The lesson: Don't grow too much of things you (or your family) don't like.

She said Maybe it's just me, but everything tastes better deep-fried. I should have shared my parsnip chip recipe with Steve.

She said Tomatoes are such a challenge in Calgary, so I finally built a greenhouse. I still grow a few tomatoes on the deck or in pots on the hot side of the house but the main crop is definitely under cover.

Lots of varieties to choose from: cabbages (left) and lettuce (right).

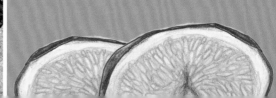

Clockwise: early crops include broad
beans; lettuce ; radish; and spinach.

Coaches' Thumbs-Up Guide: 10 Crops for an Early Spring Start
For gardeners who are keen to have as long a season of fresh garden veg
as possible, here are 10 crops well suited to an early spring start:

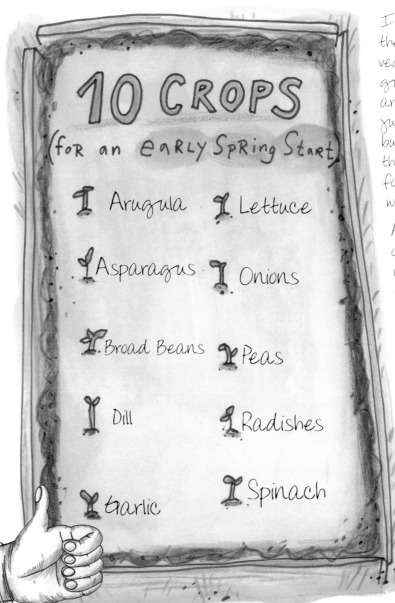

10 CROPS (for an EaRLY SPRing Start)

1. Arugula
1. Lettuce
1. Asparagus
1. Onions
1. Broad Beans
1. Peas
1. Dill
1. Radishes
1. Garlic
1. Spinach

She said

I just don't have the space for big vegetable plants that don't give back. A mammoth artichoke plant may give just one artichoke-so I just buy these space-wasters at the market. Instead, I focus on things that really work for me, like carrots!

A friend tells the story of her community garden where members decided to plant broad beans...but at the end of the summer, they realized nobody ate broad beans. Even the food bank turned them away. Oops. Meanwhile, my daughter Kalen insists broad beans are her favourite veggie.

Coaches' Thumbs-Up Guide: 10 Crops you can Harvest After the First Fall Frost

The warning of a first fall frost sends vegetable gardeners scurrying to pick all of the tomatoes, peppers, eggplants, cucumbers, and other frost-sensitive produce in the garden. With the crops below, you don't have to worry about light frost: just leave them in the garden.

10 CROPS

1. Arugula
2. Beets
3. Broccoli (and its relatives, including Brussels sprouts)
4. Carrots
5. Celery
6. Leeks
7. Parsley
8. Parsnips
9. Swiss chard
10. Turnips

> **She said** What about potatoes? You can pull them out of the ground up to the first killing frost and they store for weeks after that with no special attention.

Coaches' Thumbs-Up Guide: Three Vegetable Garden Must-Haves 3

1. **Carrots.** Try carrots because once you have tasted a fresh, sweet carrot straight from the ground, you'll feel pumped about your vegetable garden.

2. **Swiss Chard.** Grow this crop because, unlike lettuce and spinach, which produce for a short while and are then no longer edible, Swiss chard just keeps on going all season long. You can continually cut back the leaves and it will keep on producing well into the fall.

3. **Tomatoes.** There are countless interesting tomato varieties you can grow, from pink to yellow to red, from round to teardrop to egg-shaped. With all the hype about a Mediterranean diet, fresh tomatoes have become must-haves.

> **He said** Another reason to grow tomatoes is the bragging rights...guys bragging to other guys.

> **She said** Make that four must-haves. I like one or two celery plants because most of my recipes call for one or two stalks and having the plants in the garden saves me a trip to the store. Celery is often cited as a crop likely to have pesticide residue.

> **She said** OK, make that five must-haves. I can never buy enough small fresh zucchini in season. Yes the big ones are sold at markets and some smaller ones are sold at big-box stores, but a tender homegrown zucchini is a thing of beauty.

> Pumpkins waste space so they are probably the only vegetable not on my "must-have" list, although I have grown one for my grandchildren. Yes, my plant last year only grew one pumpkin. Go figure.

MORE ON POSH SQUASH

Not sure what to call the fancy, posh-looking summer squashes that are once again the darlings of the culinary scene? You're not alone.

The squash name neurotica stems from a tangle of things: there are three main species, but each species has a number of varieties; all these varieties are more commonly classed by use, shape, and time of harvest than by their species; classification categories overlap; and, to top it off, there are regional differences in names. Wow.

It's enough to befuddle the aspiring squash grower, who must remember that a zucchini is a summer squash, but not all summer squash are zucchini!

Clockwise: later crops include sunflowers; beets; leeks; and broccoli.

MORE ON POSH SQUASH

Squash by Time of Harvest

WHAT	HARVEST	INCIDENTALLY
Summer Squash	Harvested immature so rind and seeds are still tender and edible.	Often eaten raw or lightly cooked.
Winter Squash	Harvested mature so will store well.	Usually eaten well cooked. The well-known acorn squash is also known as a pepper squash—and often confused with the butternut squash.

Summer Squash by Shape

WHAT	FEATURES	INCIDENTALLY
Crook neck	Club-shaped, with a narrow, crook neck at the stem end.	Yellow skin may be bumpy or smooth.
Papaya / Pear	Shaped like a…papaya.	Yellow skin is smooth.
Straight neck	Straight neck is narrower at stem end.	Yellow skin may be bumpy or smooth.
Scallops	Disc shaped with scalloped edges.	Skin may be yellow, blue, green, or white. These varieties are also known as pattypan varieties.

Summer Squash: Zucchinis and Marrows

WHAT	FEATURES	INCIDENTALLY
Zucchini	Cylindrical shape with smooth skin that is usually green or yellow. Flesh is white.	Also known as courgette. Often picked when small, 10–15 cm (4–6 inches). Just to make things confusing…there are round zucchinis too.
Marrow (English)	Cylindrical shape, with skin that is usually very pale. Flesh slightly greenish.	Also known as vegetable marrow. Usually picked when full size.
Marrow (Italian)	Similar to English marrow, but with stripes.	Also known as cocozelle.
Cousa (Lebanese zucchini)	Slightly oval shape, with skin that is pale green.	A zucchini popular in the Middle East, where it is often stuffed and baked.

She said I cook summer squash at any stage, big or small. Favourite winter squash include butternut and spaghetti.

He said Note for gadget-loving Donna: there's a special tool used to hollow out cousa so they can be stuffed. And I have it!

My neighbour Joe, who is originally from Malta, grows round zucchini suitable for stuffing and baking. Joe and I often compare notes on the rabbit terrorism taking place in our gardens.

From top: wow guests with Sungold tomatoes; colourful carrots; garlic chives.

CROP	WHY TRY	INCIDENTALLY
Asparagus	Produces spears every spring at a time when there is not a lot ready in the garden—and takes care of itself once established.	Widely available as year-old plants that can be harvested sooner than plants started from seed.
Sorrel	A great addition to spring salads and can be cooked into tangy sauces or soups.	Pick it as soon as leaves appear.
Rhubarb	Doesn't protest about lousy growing conditions—and lasts forever.	Technically a vegetable, though most people use it in the kitchen as a fruit.

FORCING RHUBARB

To keep rhubarb patches tip-top, it's a good idea to divide rhubarb clumps every few years and then enrich the soil with compost.

Now you have an extra clump, which can be forced in the late winter or early spring. Not only do you get extra early rhubarb—it's very pink, sweet, and tender too.

SEASON	WHAT TO DO
Fall	Divide your clump before the ground freezes, but after the leaves have died back.
Winter	Store the root in any sort of container. Keep it cold—it can freeze. Forget about it!
Late Winter / Spring	Now it's time to force it. Put it somewhere warm and preferably dark. Water as needed. You will get pink and very tender rhubarb stalks.

Rhubarb in the cold cupboard in February.

He said Long-lasting is an understatement: the rhubarb patch at my previous house had been there for decades.

She said Thomas Leo Ogren, author of Allergy Free Gardening, told me to avoid male-only asparagus plants: the pollen is linked to a higher incidence of allergies.

Buying male-only plants means no self-seeding and spreading of asparagus seeds in the garden.

From left: colourful pole beans and gherkins; heirloom tomatoes; dahlias; baby-size carrots; and bronze fennel.

He sai

Coaches' Thumbs-Up Guide: 7 Crops To Make Guests Say Wow

Half the fun of growing veggies is sharing them with other people. And when you have guests who are excited about your garden produce—or when you go to a potluck and people ooh and ah, then growing vegetables becomes especially satisfying.

Here are some not-too-mainstream-yet vegetables that are sure to elicit glowing feedback.

She said I love the newest hybrid tomatoes like Sungold-sweet, almost disease-free and early too.

He said When I had too many Mexican gherkins to eat fresh, I brined some along with garlic and dill, with delicious results.

CROP	WHY THE WoW
Beans (pole)	With many pole bean varieties being a bit longer and flatter than bush beans—and with yellow and purple varieties too—imagine a veggie platter with raw, crunchy, colourful beans that are perfect for dipping. Colour is a big part of the wow (the purple colour disappears when you cook them) so serve them raw.
Carrots	Again, colour is the trick. Carrots come in white, yellow, red—even purple. Serve an assortment of colours, either fresh or cooked, and watch for the smiles on the faces of eaters.
Dahlia	No, it's not a typo. Yes, dahlia is an annual flower. But it also has an edible root—and we have market gardener David Cohlmeyer to thank for putting us onto this "wow" crop.
Fennel	In addition to Florence fennel, with an edible bulb, there's bronze fennel grown for the beautiful foliage, which dresses up a plate beautifully. And then there's the flowers on both bronze and Florence fennel— airy light yellow clusters sure to elicit questions and enhance salads.
Ground Cherries	Though technically a fruit, the ground cherry deserves a place in the vegetable garden. People love to unhusk the cloaked fruit—and then smile as they enjoy its pineapple-like zing.
Mexican Gherkins	Size matters. In this case, the size is small, as Mexican gherkins (also known as mouse melons) are small, fingernail-sized, pop-in-your-mouth novelties for guests.
Tomatoes	Stripes, splotches, striations...tomatoes will give you a patterned delight to make guests say "wow." Add to that varied flavours, and an assortment of tomatoes is very worthwhile.

Meet The Extended Family In The Onion Clan

Meet the onion clan members, who we can classify many ways: by colour, size, pungency, keeping quality, maturity date, and day length required for bulb formation. Some varieties, such as Bermuda onions, are associated with specific regions. In the northern half of North America, where summer days are longer, look for long-day varieties; and in the southern half, for short-day varieties.

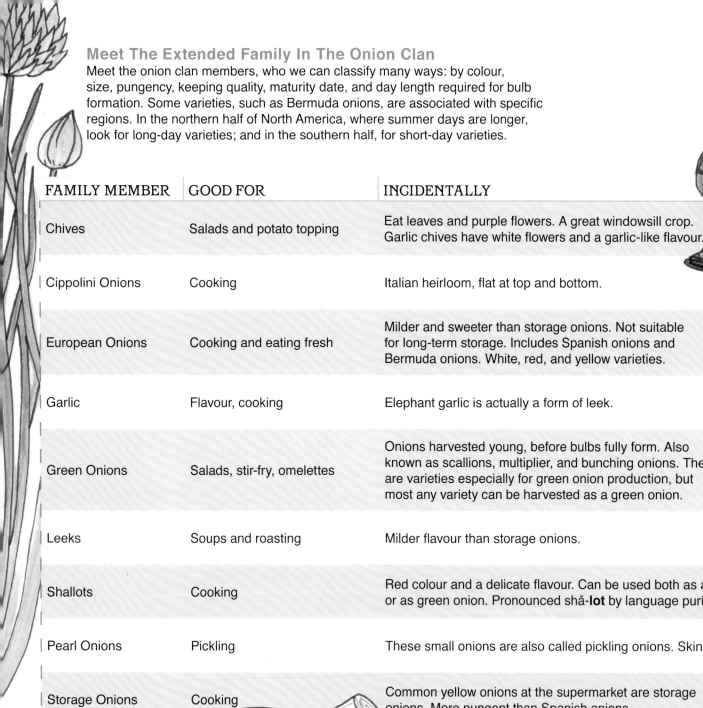

FAMILY MEMBER	GOOD FOR	INCIDENTALLY
Chives	Salads and potato topping	Eat leaves and purple flowers. A great windowsill crop. Garlic chives have white flowers and a garlic-like flavour.
Cippolini Onions	Cooking	Italian heirloom, flat at top and bottom.
European Onions	Cooking and eating fresh	Milder and sweeter than storage onions. Not suitable for long-term storage. Includes Spanish onions and Bermuda onions. White, red, and yellow varieties.
Garlic	Flavour, cooking	Elephant garlic is actually a form of leek.
Green Onions	Salads, stir-fry, omelettes	Onions harvested young, before bulbs fully form. Also known as scallions, multiplier, and bunching onions. There are varieties especially for green onion production, but most any variety can be harvested as a green onion.
Leeks	Soups and roasting	Milder flavour than storage onions.
Shallots	Cooking	Red colour and a delicate flavour. Can be used both as a dry bulb or as green onion. Pronounced shǎ-**lot** by language purists.
Pearl Onions	Pickling	These small onions are also called pickling onions. Skins are white.
Storage Onions	Cooking	Common yellow onions at the supermarket are storage onions. More pungent than Spanish onions.

THUMBS DOWN: FAILURE TO WOW

She said My daughter Kalen talks about the asparagus peas she grew in Edmonton: "They grew really well and were quite pretty with their bright red flowers but the pods themselves (even at a very immature stage) were woody and pulpy and tasted neither like asparagus nor peas. It was confusing, and the whole row ultimately ended up in the compost heap after some very unsuccessful culinary attempts. Maybe there are special preparation techniques that need to be employed to bring out their flavour and texture in a pleasing way, but for my money, and garden space, regular garden peas are by far the champion. In the process of 'editing' the garden over time, asparagus peas were not even considered for a second chance."

He said I, too, tried these, and they were tough and woody for me. Thumbs down.

MENU SUBSTITUTION SPINACH SUB PLEASE

At risk of offending spinach lovers everywhere, let's just say that fresh garden spinach is a true treat, but growing it can be…bothersome. You see, summer and long days makes it obsessed with flowering and setting seed, which result in leather leaves. So we'd like to throw out some spinach substitutes for you to try in the garden in between the ideal spinach seasons of spring and fall.

SPINACH SUB	INCIDENTALLY
Amaranth	Also called Chinese spinach. Related to the weed pigweed—which is also used sometimes as a spinach sub.
Arugula	In early spring and fall usually germinates more quickly than spinach.
Beet Leaves	Tolerates warm weather. Not obsessed with flowering like spinach—and, of course, roots are edible too.
Corn Salad (Mâche)	Likes cold weather, so from a weather perspective, similar to spinach and not the best sub.
Malabar Spinach	Glossy, reddish leaves on an attractive climbing vine. Highly ornamental. Hates the cold.
Miner's Lettuce	Also known as claytonia. Highly cold tolerant.
Mizuna	Tolerates cold and frost. Deeply serrated leaves are very attractive. Peppery flavour.
New Zealand Spinach	Also called tetragonia. Loves the warmth—hates the cold—and will not bolt in hot weather.
Orach	Attractive leaves. Plants come in red, yellow, and green varieties.
Swiss Chard	Use stalk on large leaves instead of bamboo shoots in stir-fry recipes. Tolerates warm weather. Not obsessed with flowering.
Weeds!	Lamb's Quarters is a cousin of spinach, and many claim that, harvested young, it's a good substitute.

Still have your heart set on growing spinach? Bloomsdale is an old, dependable, open-pollinated variety. Market gardener David Cohlmeyer—who has grown a lot of spinach—says it is still the best variety.

She said Thumbs down for the New Zealand spinach. There is a bitter aftertaste that stays in the throat.

He said My hands-down favourite spinach sub is Swiss chard.

MENU SUBSTITUTION NO-SWEAT CROPS PLEASE

Savvy diners aren't shy about asking for a menu substitution at a restaurant if what's offered doesn't suit them. Here are examples of low-sweat, labour-saving substitutions you can employ in the garden.

ON THE MENU	NO-SWEAT SUB	THE RATIONALE
Bush Beans	Pole Beans	It's no less work planting pole beans—but when it comes to harvest, pole beans can entail a lot less bending and kneeling. Plant them against a fence so there's no need to bother with stakes.
Cauliflower	Broccoli	Not only is cauliflower more finicky, to get snow-white heads it must be blanched, which is often done by holding the leaves over the head with an elastic. It's a lot of bother compared to broccoli, which requires no blanching. Sprouting broccoli is even easier than regular broccoli.
Sweet Potato	Squash	Squash is so much less work. Instead of transplanting sweet potato plants, you just poke squash seeds into the soil. And—here's the biggie—instead of digging out sweet potato roots, you just snip squash from the vine. You still get the sweet, orange ingredient for baking.

Vegetables from Seed versus Transplants

Some types of vegetable plants grow best when sown directly in the vegetable garden. But in many cases, it is beneficial to grow the vegetable seeds indoors, and then transplant them into the garden. For plants such as pepper, tomato, eggplant, Brussels sprouts, leeks, and celery we do this because, in our relatively short season, there is not enough time to grow them from seed in the garden and get a decent harvest.

Other plants, such as lettuce, broccoli, cauliflower, cabbage, cucumber, and zucchini, can be sown directly in the garden—but starting transplants indoors gives the gardener a jump on the season.

DEFINITION: TRANSPLANT.

Transplant is a term used for young plants that are grown from seed to be later planted in the vegetable garden. Some transplants are started indoors during the winter, while others are started in a "nursery" bed in the garden.

SEED TERMINOLOGY

Heirlooms are older varieties that have become less common as commercial producers switch to newer ones. Many gardeners choose heirlooms for historical interest or novel colours or flavours—and many people are concerned about preserving the genetic diversity found in such varieties.

[he said] I grow a tomato variety given to me by my father's cousin, whose father got it from an Italian neighbour named Franco, who brought it from the old country. For me, the Franco tomato is an heirloom because it has been passed from generation to generation, and it has a story.

[she said] My daughter Kalen grows her mother-in-law's beans, brought over from Bosnia. She now saves them herself.

Hybrids are nothing more than a cross between two varieties of the same plant: think of a cockapoo dog, a hybrid of a cocker spaniel and poodle. Along with improved vigour, hybrids can have traits such as improved yield, flavour, colour, and disease resistance. But...they do not yield seeds that are likely to resemble the parents.

Open-Pollinated varieties are stable, non-hybrid varieties giving seed that grow into plants like the parent. Cross-pollination by wind or insects can happen. See page 62 for more about self-fertile crops that come "true."

Organic: Grown following organic standards on land certified as organic by an accredited organization.

Top left: peppers are started indoors as transplants; cauliflower (top right) is more work than broccoli (middle); try squash as a sub for sweet potatoes (bottom left).

Pelleted Seeds: These have been coated so that the size of the seed is large and uniform and easy to plant by machine or a small child. Some seeds are so expensive they are coated to prevent loss in shipping and handling.

Treated Seeds are coated with protectants such as fungicides to control diseases that hamper germination or kill young seedlings. If the seed is pink, good chance it is treated.

[She said] Treated seed is not for the organic gardener-the "treatment, depending upon what it is, may kill both good and bad fungi.

I'm not ethically opposed to treated seed. It's not inconsistent with my preference for a sterile seeding mix indoors. Let's put things into perspective: If I use foot powder for athlete's foot, it controls the disease and also probably kills some good microbes on my skin... but hey, that's life. If you take our advice to try a cheater row of beans in a cold spring (page 21.), there's a decent likelihood of the combination of cold soil and rot organisms killing the seed—and in this case, I would recommend treated seed. *[He said]*

[She said] If Steve is worried about bad soil microbes, he needs to use compost tea to build in a natural defence system with good microbes.

Untreated Seeds haven't been treated with fungicides. While some untreated seeds may be organic, untreated is not the same thing as organic.

GMO DEMYSTIFIED

Let's step back for a second to point out that lingo can be a stumbling block. What in some parts of the world is called genetically modified (GM) or genetically modified organism (GMO) is defined by the Canadian Food Inspection Agency (which reports to the federal minister of agriculture) as genetically engineered (GE).

❋ Genetically Engineered (GE): modified using techniques that permit the direct transfer or removal of genes, including recombinant DNA techniques.

❋ Transgenic: You might have heard about a tomato with fish genes a few years back. That is what can be considered "transgenic," and it is a subset of the broader class of GE (or what many people know as GMO). While that tomato was a commercial flop, a transgenic, GE crop in common use today is BT corn, which has genetic material from a bacterium. *[He said]*

Here's some trivia for you: the Canadian regulatory system does not regulate GE plants. That's because it doesn't regulate the breeding process—but instead regulates the final outcome, and any plants considered to have "new" traits are regulated.

[She said] Overall, though, gardeners are distrustful of anything with so little testing and because GMOs can't be certified as organic and can get mixed in with the gene pool of non-GMO seed, this gardener is trying to stay away from them.

[He said] For me the bigger issue for people to think about is that the development of new crops has shifted away from government agencies and into the realm of large, multinational companies.

Save Your Own Seeds
Deciding What To Save

You can save your own seed for many of the vegetables in your garden... but you're undertaking a lot if you want to save all your own seeds.

He said I save my own tomato seeds, and encourage lettuce to self-seed in the garden. And I save seeds of hard-to-find crops such as the Mexican gherkins that my kids love. But I don't try to save seeds of everything...for me it is not practical.

She said Guess what? I generally like buying seed.

Crops That Come "True"

Without delving into botany, it's enough to say that some open-pollinated crops, such as tomatoes, will usually come "true" from seed. That simply means that you can cut apart a tomato, save the seeds—and when you grow them, get more of the same tomatoes. That's because these crops are self-fertile (meaning pollen from a given flower can pollinate that same flower).

Self-seeding dill becomes a "weed."

Other crops give seeds that are unlikely to yield the same sort of squash as that from which they came. Such crops—which cross-pollinate—are receptive to pollen moved by insects and wind. If you're after a plant that resembles the parent...don't bother saving these. If you really want to save the seeds, grow just one variety and hope that there are no pollen transfers.

From left: lettuce and spinach readily reseed.

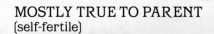

MOSTLY TRUE TO PARENT (self-fertile)	NOT TRUE TO PARENT (require cross-pollinating)
beans, lettuce, peas, peppers, spinach, tomatoes	broccoli, cabbage, corn, cucumbers, leeks, melon, radishes, squash, turnip, zucchini

Annuals, Biennials, or Perennials

Many garden vegetables are annuals—meaning that you can expect seeds the year of planting.

But that's not the case with everything. Some crops, known as biennials, don't hit the reproductive stage until year two. Beets and carrots are a good example. In the limited space of the home vegetable garden, you'll want to consider whether you have sufficient space to grow biennials for two years just for seeds. We don't.

SOME ANNUALS	SOME BIENNIALS
beans, broccoli, corn, dill, cucumbers, eggplant, lettuce, melons, peas, radish, spinach, squash	beets, Brussels sprouts, cabbage, carrots, cauliflower, celery, kale, kohlrabi, leeks, onion, parsley, parsnip, rutabaga, Swiss chard

She said Swiss chard may be a biennial but under heat and water stress it will produce seed in the first year. OK-don't ask how I know that.

He said Don't worry. I stressed out my beet plants this year and they went to seed. Oops!

From top: save seeds of unusual plants such as Mexican gherkins; green pea seed is dried in the pod then shelled and dried further; whole potatoes are saved for "seed."

How To Save And Store Seed

Harvest seeds from healthy, early, and productive plants. Ideally, let an early specimen set seed instead of waiting until fall, when plants slow down and you might have missed the best opportunity for seed.

He said To commercial seed houses, seed free from dried bits of pod, stem, and leaves is important. But as a home gardener, I don't fuss with picking out all the bits. Who cares?

PLANT TYPE	WHEN TO HARVEST
Fruits (e.g. tomatoes, cucumbers, peppers, squash)	Select those that are fully ripe, but not rotten.
Podded crops (e.g. beans, peas, radish)	Allow to become very dry for harvest. Light frost won't harm bean pods that are dry. Dry peas and beans until they can't be dented with a fingernail.
Seed heads (e.g. carrots, dill)	Usually become brown and papery.

While drying seeds, warm conditions with good air circulation are best. If you're drying them outdoors, remember that there is often overnight dew in late summer and fall—so bring them indoors overnight.

Once it's time to store them through the winter, you want to have conditions that prevent the growth of microbes and don't encourage premature germination. That typically means cool and dry. Dampness is what you want to avoid, as it can lead to rot.

SEED LONGEVITY	CROP
Up to 2 years	corn, okra, onions, parsley, parsnip
3–4 years	beans, carrots, celery, leeks, lettuce, peas, pepper, spinach, tomatoes
5–6 years	beets, broccoli, cabbage, cauliflower, cucumber, melon, radishes, squash, Swiss chard

He said I smear the inside of the tomato (the part containing seeds) on a paper towel and let it dry. That's all—except I have to pick them off the paper towel in the spring.

She said If you want to gradually "select" your own strain of early-ripening tomatoes, make sure to save the earliest ripe fruits each year. Of course I think about this every year, but somehow the first fruits get gobbled up right in the garden!

Buying Seed

Mail Order

Seed houses are firms that sell seeds to growers and homeowners. They are like the department stores of the seed world. For the most part, they don't produce the seed they sell: they merely package and distribute it.

You will also find smaller seed houses that specialize in niche markets such as organics and heirloom varieties. Some, but not all, of these will produce their own seed.

How do you pick a seed company? Most will send you a free catalogue. Look them up on the Internet, request a catalogue, and then compare prices, varieties, and shipping charges.

Seed Exchanges

Heritage (heirloom) seeds are not always commercialized. While some seed houses sell them, many varieties can also be found at seed exchanges (such as Seedy Saturdays). These are fun gathering points for information and seed exchange.

Choose Varieties Suited to Your Climate

Not all vegetable varieties are created equal: flavour and appearance aside, some grow more quickly than others do. Many seed packets and catalogues show the number of days to harvest, which is not a precise number but, rather, a comparative one.

The heat and length of day in your area will probably have more effect on the suitability of a variety than the actual number of frost-free days. For example, when two plants are grown at the same latitude, the one grown on a roof will grow or ripen quicker than one grown in the ground—because of the warmer temperatures on the roof.

While earlier varieties—those that are ready to harvest sooner—make sense in areas with a shorter growing season, don't rule out other varieties.

When planting peas, for example, you can plant varieties with different harvest dates, so your harvest is staggered. This results in an extended harvest. Use first- and last-frost dates to gauge approximately how many growing days you have in your area. But more importantly, talk to experienced gardeners to find out what varieties they grow.

From left: parsnip leaves look a bit like celery; include beans in a rotation to boost soil nitrogen levels; rotate tomatoes from year to year.

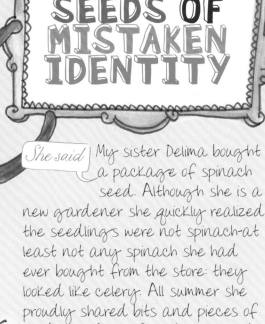

SEEDS OF MISTAKEN IDENTITY

She said My sister Delima bought a package of spinach seed. Although she is a new gardener she quickly realized the seedlings were not spinach-at least not any spinach she had ever bought from the store: they looked like celery. All summer she proudly shared bits and pieces of her "celery" with friends who used it in their soups and stews and other dishes. With the arrival of fall, Delima's husband dug up what was left of the garden and quickly discovered the "celery" was actually parsnips, huge and white even after all her leaf harvesting! She proudly delivered a parsnip to me for a fall stew.

Crop Rotation Protestation

We don't see eye to eye on crop rotation. We both agree that the concept is sound—is logical—is excellent. But that's where it ends.

So we might have called this section a rotation capitulation, with Donna, a devotee of the practice, and Steve, the naysayer, coming to agree that, yes, we owe it to readers to give it a section.

He said In our ode to guff we talk about what makes sense to a scientist can be "dumb" in the garden. I think rotation in tight urban spots fits the bill.

Some vegetable farms—and some vegetable gardeners—"rotate" crops so that no one crop or crop family is in the same spot two years in a row. Many have rotation cycles that stretch more than two years… often up to four and even five years.

This dance of the crops is not an aesthetical whim nor is it based on guff. It's based on the following:

- Some crops suck more nutrients from the soil than others.
- Some crops actually put nutrients into the soil.
- Pest populations may increase when a crop is grown more than one year in the same spot.
- The probability of disease for some crops is increased when a crop is on the same spot for more than one year.

The challenge for home gardeners is that a four- or five-year rotation probably isn't in the works. There's not enough space. At the very least, home gardeners should rotate where they grow root crops, legumes, and the "needy" members of the cabbage family.

Can't Fit In Multi-Year Rotations? Try This.

Plant a green manure crop in the fall—or during the summer or spring wherever there is a bit of empty space. You are doing two things:

- Adding organic matter to cheer on your soil microbes
- Breaking disease and insect cycles

And by cheering on those microbes, remember, you're also unlocking soil nutrients for crops.

That Needy Cabbage Family

We all suffer from fondness for certain foods, and cabbage family members are no exception. But to compound the matter, the "family," as we will call the various cabbages, does not team up with mychorrizal fungi in the soil as most other vegetables do: That's like putting a lock on the fridge door.

Meanwhile, cabbage clan members are attacked by the same mafia of pests including flea beetles, cabbage worms, root maggots, and aphids. So don't just rotate cabbages and broccoli out of one spot—rotate the whole family.

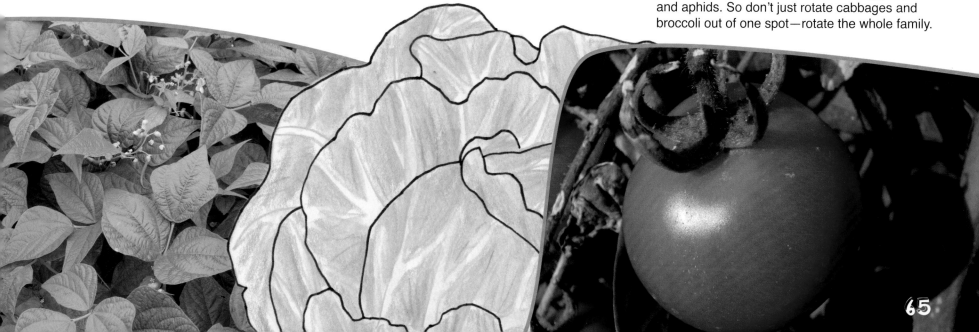

Who belongs to the needy cabbage family? Here are some members of this well-known clan:

- Broccoli
- Bok choy
- Brussels sprouts
- Cauliflower
- Kale
- Kohlrabi
- Rapini
- Red, Savoy, & Chinese cabbage

Mix Families To Keep The Buffet Stocked

If you're still digesting the concept that different crops feed on soil nutrients…differently, think of a buffet restaurant: The plant family with all the kids will quickly empty the French-fry section of the buffet; the mid-life, weight-watching plants grimace as they deplete the low-fat dishes; and the brawny muscle-building types of the plant world selectively pass by low-fat stuff and gobble up all the high-fat, high-protein fare.

In a garden scenario, where we plant rows or blocks of these families, the favoured foods might be gone—gobbled up—after a season or two. But if we put in the fry-loving family after the weight-watching ones have gobbled up the low-fat grub… nobody is going to complain, right?

Different crops (and crop families) consume different amounts of basic elements such as boron, calcium, molybdenum, magnesium, and manganese. If we rotate through those crops, it's like moving our buffet patrons from spot to spot along the buffet.

❝

Rotation Simplified

Here is a simple rotation in which you have four designated garden areas through which you rotate your crops.

He said My parting advice? Don't get stressed out about crop rotation. Yes, in principle it's great…and crop rotation is an important aspect of sustainable commercial farming. But it's highly impractical in a small, home garden where the area ideal for tomatoes one year probably overlaps with the area where you grow them the next.

With just a few plants of each crop, the likelihood of a buildup of pests or disease is minimal compared to commercial production.

Healthy soil grows healthier plants, which in turn can better deal with the pest and disease pressures that NOT rotating causes. So if you're suffering rotation consternation, focus on your soil.

Don't complain to me if your **She said** *tomatoes get blossom end rot from lack of calcium if you don't rotate your tomatoes. Be prepared to add supplements.*

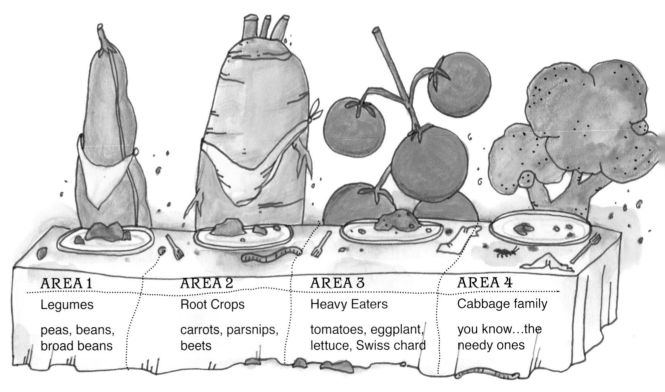

AREA 1	AREA 2	AREA 3	AREA 4
Legumes	Root Crops	Heavy Eaters	Cabbage family
peas, beans, broad beans	carrots, parsnips, beets	tomatoes, eggplant, lettuce, Swiss chard	you know…the needy ones

Crop Selection
Guff Busted

Guff Says

Hybrid seeds are bad and heirlooms are good.

GUFFAWERS RESPOND

If you want to save your own seeds, hybrids aren't the way to go because you must buy them from a seed retailer. That's a no-brainer.

But it doesn't mean that hybrids are inherently bad. We're not talking about fish genes in a tomato here: we're talking about two lines of a plant that are crossed to give a variety with desirable traits.

She said I garden in Calgary, where the tomato season is short at best, and I've had mixed results with heirloom varieties of tomatoes, which are late to produce. So I'm eager to try new vegetable varieties, including early hybrids, every year.

Guff Says

Seeds from a "local" retailer are best suited to your climate.

GUFFAWERS RESPOND

Certainly, support local businesses. And if you have local seed retailers with locally adapted varieties, then definitely try those. But remember this:

- Most commercially grown seeds are produced in warmer climates where two or more generations can be raised in a single season.

- A specific variety will have the same characteristics whether raised nearby or far away.

Where do local retailers really shine? Many have test gardens where they trial and showcase the varieties they distribute. Based on those trials they can pick regionally suited varieties.

By the way, we both order seeds from around the world if we find something neat.

Crop Selection Q&A

If I keep seed packages, must they be stored in the fridge?

No. It is true that storing seed in a cool, dark place extends the storage life. We suggest using an old coffee can or a well-sealed plastic container. Leave the seeds in the original packets, write the date on the packet, and keep the container somewhere fairly cool and dark. If you have space in the fridge, that's great—but who does?

Real Vegetable Gardeners Don't...

Real vegetable gardeners don't feel shame if they buy transplants instead of growing from seed.

Life is busy and gardeners may not have a good spot to start seeds indoors. If you do—great. If you can't or don't want to—don't sweat it. The best way to get just a few plants for a small garden is to buy transplants rather than packets of 20-plus seeds.

Real vegetable gardeners don't limit themselves to plants their parents knew and grew.

Check out the exotic array available in local and distant catalogues and try something new every spring.

She said I just can't grow warm-season crops in my cold Calgary climate. I do not try to grow okra, eggplant, artichoke, or tomatillos, but just a few miles north in warmer Edmonton my daughter easily grows tomatillos and often gets eggplants. My advice? As my daughter proved to me, if you really want to grow it, you should try it—at least once.

TO: STEVE

67

Difficulty legend: TESTY / DOABLE / EASY

Crop Name + Picture	Worth it?	Difficulty	How Much?	Seeds	Where to Grow	Seeding...
Artichoke (globe)	Nope / Nope		A whole field			Indoors, 9–10 weeks before last frost.
Arugula	Yep! / Yep!		Up to 1 packet			Outdoors, as soon as soil can be worked—or earlier in a hotbed.
Asparagus	Yep! / Yep!		A half dozen plants per person			Instead of growing from seed, buy roots to save a couple of years.
Beans (broad)	Nope / Yep!		Up to 1 packet			Outdoors, as soon as soil can be worked.
Beans (bush, dry, pole)	Yep! / Yep!		Up to 1 packet			Outdoors, after last frost, till mid-summer.
Beets	Yep! / Yep!		Up to 1 packet			Outdoors, as soon as soil can be worked, till early summer.
Broccoli	Yep! / Yep!		3–6 plants			Indoors, 6–7 weeks before last frost. Outdoors, 2 weeks before last frost.
Brussels Sprouts	Yep! / Yep!		3–6 plants			Indoors, 10–12 weeks before last frost.
Cabbage	Nope / Nope		3–6 plants			Indoors, 4–6 weeks before last frost. Outdoors, 2 weeks before last frost.
Cardoon	Yep! / Nope		1–2 plants			Indoors, 9–10 weeks before last frost.

TRANSPLANT OUTSIDE	T.L.C.	PROBLEMS	Incidentally...
After danger of frost.	Give this heavy feeder rich soil.	Usually bears in second year, so you must trick plants by exposing them to a cold treatment.	Come on— who's got enough space for this crop? A very inconsistent crop for me.
N/A	Not needed.	Best grown early, before pesky flea beetles arrive and fill the leaves with holes.	Great succession crop.
Plant roots as soon as soil can be worked.	Top dress with compost every year to add fertility and keep down weeds.	Asparagus beetle.	You probably won't grow enough.
N/A	Plants require support.	Aphids, aphids, aphids. Keep an eye on shoot tips.	Sometimes called horse beans…an appropriate name for these large, dry, and mealy things. A gift for gardeners because they can be planted so early!
N/A	Stake pole beans, or plant near a fence. Regular picking prolongs harvest.	Best picked when plants are dry. Otherwise, you are tempting the disease gods.	Love the mixed seed packets of yellow, green, and purple beans. Be daring…try planting "cheater" seeds outdoors 2 weeks before the last frost.
N/A	Plants die if they dry out while sprouting.	Leaf spots are common, though don't affect edibility.	May grow decently with some shade. Try a couple of varieties. I like the large cylindrical ones that store well.
Hardened off transplants can tolerate some frost.	Cover with fine netting (row covers) to keep out bugs.	Cabbage moth larvae eat and poop on uncovered plants.	Cover for the bugs. Cover? I like varieties with small florets…so if bugs spoil some, there are lots of others to pick from.
Hardened off transplants can tolerate some frost.	Pinch out tip in late summer to direct energy towards sprouts. Remove lower leaves in August.	Aphids – especially late in fall.	Hybrids rule! (And they produce better too.) Some say treat as broccoli, but an earlier start is better.
Hardened off transplants can tolerate some frost.	Cover with netting.	Bugs! If you don't cover them, they become the sacrificial plants in the garden.	Red cabbage and Savoy are pretty. Cabbage is cheap to buy, a space hog, and terribly bug prone.
Tolerates some frost.	Rich soil for this heavy feeder. To blanch leaf stalks, tie a piece of cardboard around the base of the plant.	Once harvesting begins, with lower leaves picked first, upper leaves can collapse… so tie lightly with twine.	Beauty. Queen of the garden—and also great in risotto and soups. Takes a lot of space for a few measly stalks.

Difficulty legend: TESTY / DOABLE / EASY

CROP NAME + PICTURE	WORTH it?	Difficulty	How Much?	Seeds	Where to Grow	Seeding...
Carrots	Yep! / Yep!	(testy)	2+ packets		☀️	Outdoors, as soon as soil can be worked.
Cauliflower	Yep! / Nope	(doable)	3–6 plants		☀️	Indoors, 4–6 weeks before last frost.
Celery (root)	Nope / Yep!	(doable)	3–6 plants		☀️	Indoors, 10–12 weeks before last frost.
Celery (stalk + leaf)	Yep! / Yep!	(doable)	2–4 plants		☀️	Indoors, 10–12 weeks before last frost.
Corn	Nope / Nope	(doable)	1 packet		☀️	Indoors, 4 weeks before last frost. / Outdoors, around last frost.
Corn Salad (mache)	Nope / Nope	(easy)	1 packet		☀️/⛅	Outdoors, 2 weeks before last frost.
Cucumber	Yep! / Yep!	(doable)	½ packet		☀️/⛅	Indoors, 4 weeks before last frost. / Outdoors, after last frost.
Dill	Yep! / Yep!	(easy)	½ packet		☀️/⛅	Outdoors, as soon as soil can be worked, or in the fall.
Eggplant	Nope / Yep!	(testy)	6 plants		☀️	Indoors, 10 weeks before last frost.
Fennel	Yep! / Yep!	(doable)	1 packet		☀️	Indoors, 4 weeks before last frost. / Outdoors, after last frost.

	TRANSPLANT OUTSIDE	T.L.C.	PROBLEMS	Incidentally...
20	N/A	Water and thin for bigger carrots.	Carrot rust fly larvae make tunnels in the carrots. Avoid soils recently enriched with manure or face hairy carrots.	Co-plant with radish to get the spacing right and prevent soil from crusting.
9	Outside a week later than broccoli.	Cover with netting. Use elastic bands to hold leaves over white curds.	Same bugs as broccoli or cabbage plus wilting in spring from root maggot.	Come on Steve: What about the pretty new orange and pink heads? Takes too much coddling.
8	1 week after last frost.	Heavy feeder.	None… so far. It's just that it must be started very early indoors.	Not a fan really.
7	1 week after last frost.	Water, water, water. Gradually hill soil or blanch by wrapping with cardboard.	Tough stalks with strong flavour from lack of water.	So crunchy and free of chemicals if home grown. Try leaf celery.
6	1–2 weeks after last frost.	Heavy feeding. Heavy watering.	Corn maggots – yuck! Animal pests love corn.	Just a big waste of space. A non-starter in the Racoon Republic of Toronto.
5	N/A	N/A	N/A	Readily reseeds. Small leaves are a bother to harvest.
4	1–2 weeks after last frost.	Try climbing types on supports or low bush plants on hills Climbers will clamber up netting and give straighter fruit.	Diseases.	I love these in the greenhouse. Luscious and crunchy.
3	N/A	If allowed to self-seed, the patch will need thinning.	N/A	This reliable annual crop will seed itself for you.
2	Well after last frost.	Best grown in pots for extra heat.	A magnet for whiteflies.	Too much work for too little fruit in a cool climate. My best luck has been in black pots—on a hot rooftop.
1	1 week after last frost.	Likes lots of water. Feed and water well.	N/A	There are leafy and bulb types. I like the ferny foliage of bronze fennel.

TESTY ○ **DOABLE** ○ **EASY** ○						

CROP NAME + PICTURE	WORTH IT?	Difficulty	How Much?	Seeds:	Where to Grow...	Seeding...
Garlic	Yep! Yep!	●	half dozen bulbs		☀	Break bulbs into cloves, and plant cloves in fall.
Kale	Yep! Yep!	●	Up to 1 packet		☀ ⛅	Outdoors, as soon as soil can be worked.
Kohlrabi	Nope Yep!	●	1 packet		☀ ⛅	Indoors, 4–6 weeks before last frost. but don't bother to start indoors. Outdoors, as soon as ground can be worked.
Leeks	Nope Yep!	○	½ packet, or buy transplants		☀	Indoors, 10–15 weeks before last frost.
Lettuce	Yep! Yep!	●	2 packets		☀ ⛅	Indoors, 4 weeks before last frost. Or, outdoors, as soon as soil can be worked
Okra	Nope Yep!	●	6 plants		☀	Indoors, 4–6 weeks before last frost.
Onions (green)	Yep! Yep!	●	Sets are easiest		☀	Seeds: Indoors, 10 weeks before last frost. Sets: plant outdoors as soon as soil can be worked.
Onion (storage)	Yep! Yep!	●	Bag of 100 "sets" (small, pre-grown bulbs).		☀	Seeds: Indoors, 10 weeks before last frost. Sets: plant outdoors as soon as soil can be worked.
Parsley	Yep! Yep!	○	½ packet		☀ ⛅	Indoors, 10 weeks before last frost. Outdoors, as soon as soil can be worked.
Parsnips	Yep! Yep!	○	¼ packet		☀	Outdoors, as soon as soil can be worked.

TRANSPLANT OUTSIDE	T.L.C.	PROBLEMS	Incidentally...
N/A	Takes care of itself.	Bad breath.	Love these to bits. Easy to grow enough for a household for a year.
N/A	Tough as nails but tender when cooked!	N/A	I'm a latecomer to the kale party. A great crop: love the curly leaves.
N/A	None.	Because the stem, not the leaves, is harvested, doesn't need a lot of protection from insect pests.	Yes it is buggy but who cares? Nice looking plant that deserves a spot where it can be seen.
Plant out 2–4 weeks before last frost. Plant in trenches, so stalks can be buried for blanching.	Trim tops with scissors to encourage plants to thicken. Hilling plants means whiter stalks, less green.	N/A	Would love to grow these more… but season is too long. Can be harvested whenever soil is not frozen…just await a mid-winter thaw.
Stagger transplanting to stagger harvest.	N/A	Becomes bitter quickly in hot weather&so reseed regularly.	Am I just lazy or forgetful? Mine go to seed then I remember I should have reseeded sooner. Allow to self-seed, saving time and feeding the gold finches.
1 week after last frost date.	N/A	Not enough heat in many places.	Non-starter in cool soils and cool evenings! Try black pots.
Seedlings: 2–4 weeks before last frost.	Thin and use as you go.	N/A	Green onions are a great substitute for chives. Most simple way to grow? Just steal a few immature storage onions.
Seedlings: 2–4 weeks before last frost.	Water well and grow in a sunny spot for big bulbs.	Bulb rot diseases sometimes affect the crop. Don't compost affected bulbs—which are a source of disease in future years.	Intolerant of weed competition Leave half onion set out of soil to avert maggots. Rather than a dedicated patch, I use onions to fill up the sloped edge of raised beds.
N/A	Really slow to germinate… be patient.	N/A	Love the flat parsley. Try root parsley. The root stores well and adds parsley flavour to soups in winter.
N/A	Very slow to germinate. Thin till well spaced, then ignore them till the fall.	Seed loses viability very quickly: buy new seed every year.	Wow! One plant that tastes better after frost. I can say from experience that parsnip wine isn't worth the bother. Yuck.

Difficulty legend (left column): TESTY / DOABLE / EASY

CROP NAME + PICTURE	WORTH IT?	Difficulty	How Much?	Seeds:	Where to Grow...	Seeding...
Peas (Snap, Snow)	Yep! / Yep!		1 packet of each kind			Outdoors, starting as soon as soil can be worked.
Peas (Shelling)	Yep! / Yep!		1 packet			Outdoors, starting as soon as soil can be worked.
Peppers	Nope / Yep!		6–8 plants			Indoors, 10 weeks before last frost.
Potatoes	Yep! / Yep!		Minimum 5 pounds			Cut "seed" potatoes into pieces with one "eye" each.
Radishes	Yep! / Yep!		1 packet ample			Outdoors, starting as soon as soil can be worked.
Sorrel	Nope / Yep!		1–2 plants			This perennial is frost tolerant.
Spinach	Yep! / Nope		up to 1 packet			Outdoors, as soon as soil can be worked. Can also be seeded in the fall for a spring crop.
Squash (Summer)	Yep! / Yep!		1 plant of each kind			Indoors, 4 weeks before last frost. Outdoors, around the last frost date.
Squash (Winter)	Yep! / Yep!		1 plant max			Indoors, 4 weeks before last frost. Outdoors, around the last frost date.
Swiss Chard	Yep! / Yep!		1 packet			Outdoors, as soon as soil can be worked.

74

	TRANSPLANT OUTSIDE	T.L.C.	PROBLEMS	Incidentally...
20	N/A	Use netting, chicken wire, branches for climbing types.	Pick peas when plants are dry to minimize the spread of disease.	These two peas are usually staking types. Plant in cooler, shadier area to prolong harvest. Rabbits love pea seedlings.
9	N/A	Use netting, chicken wire, branches for climbing types.	Pick peas when plants are dry to minimize the spread of disease.	Summer-seeded types don't tolerate cold spring soil. You'll never grow enough! Choose a climbing variety for more prolonged yield.
8	1–2 weeks after last frost.	Pamper these plants with warmth and shelter.	Yes…many blights and bugs. This is why commercial plants are sprayed so much.	Too cold for this finicky, heat-loving crop in cooler climates. Grow in black pots.
7	Allow pieces to dry overnight. Dig a spade-deep hole in garden and place eye-side up.	Hill potatoes over growing season (or cover with leaves) to prevent green spuds.	Be wary…diseases abound.	Many varieties now available… so try something new, like blue.
16	N/A	Keep reseeding.	Flea beetles on leaves. Cracking from excess moisture.	Because it is so fast to mature, a good bedfellow for carrots, chard, and beets
15	N/A	N/A	May not overwinter in some zones.	An easy annual even if it doesn't overwinter A great lemon-flavoured leaf.
14	N/A	N/A	The harvest can be short. If conditions are hot, plants bolt and leaves become leathery…	Replanting a must…a lot of work for such a small plant. Sub with Chard Often gives barely enough to make a salad in a small space…can be a waste of space.
13	1–2 weeks after last frost.	Don't disturb roots when planting.	Learn to tell the boys from the girls. Cool weather can mean many male and no female flowers…so no fruit!	Avoid offending the sensitive roots when transplanting. Be prepared for zucchini overload… and get a zucchini bread recipe!
2	1–2 weeks after last frost.	You might need to trim plants if they grow too crazy.	Space hogs!	Choose one kind unless you have an acreage. Allow them to grow up hedges and fences.
1	Don't bother, just seed it directly.	Thin rows gradually to give more space to remaining plants.	Leaf spot or leaf miner, but just tear out damaged areas and cook.	Buy multiple packets to get great colours and better for you than beets tops Young leaves great in salad; large leaves great cooked.

75

		TESTY	DOABLE	EASY			

CROP NAME + PICTURE	WORTH it?	Difficulty	How Much?	Seeds:	Where to Grow...	Seeding...
Tomatillo	Nope Nope	○	6 plants		☀	Indoors, 4 weeks before last frost.
Tomatoes	Yep! Yep!	○	5–20 plants		☀	Indoors, 8–10 weeks before last frost.
Turnip + Rutabaga	Nope Nope	○	½ packet … maximum		☀	Outdoors, as soon as the ground can be worked. Again in August for fall crop.

1
2
3
4

SUMMARY: CROP Selection + Rotation.

Grow what you love, and love what you grow. If your chosen varieties don't perform well, make sure to try again using different varieties. Visit small seed growers who can offer unusual plants and suggestions, but try some hybrids too. Investigate online sources to find the most interesting eggplant or striped zucchini.

	TRANSPLANT OUTSIDE	T.L.C.	PROBLEMS	Incidentally...
20 / 19	2 weeks after last frost.	Allow to ramble on ground.	N/A	Better gardeners than me grow this quite well. I am jealous. I'm not crazy about the flavour.
18	1 week after last frost.	Stake, tie, prune, primp, fertilize, water, and repeat.	Cutworms. Blossom end rot. All kinds of blights and troubles but who cares? We want our tomatoes.	Cherry-sized fruit taste better. Try hybrid varieties, which often have superior disease resistance. Forget the cherry tomatoes: Grow beefsteak varieties for bragging rights!
17	N/A	N/A	Tastes yucky.	Consider buying the one rutabaga you need for Thanksgiving! Flea beetles like it…my family doesn't.

Donna and Steve's Thumbs-Up Guide

GUFF & GARDENING STUFF		DONNA	STEVE
1. Climate	Row Covers	Up	Down
	Cold Frames	Up	Up
2. Soil	Rotating Composters	Up	Down
	Rototilling	Down	Up
3. Planning	Planning Perfectionism	Down	Down
	Flowers Mixed with Veg	Up	Up
4. Garden Making	Pythagorean Theorem	Up	Down
	Double Digging	Down	Down
5. Crop Selection	Broad Beans	Down	Up
	Asparagus Pea	Down	Down
	Rotation	Up	Down

Garden Coaches Chat: No guff. Lots of fun.
for more details visit www.GardenCoachesChat.com

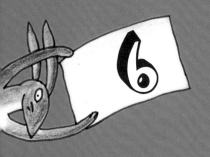
"REAL" SOIL MIXES

Older books give recipes for sterilizing garden soil in the oven. I have done this but the smell is bad! Besides, in the process, microbes and insects are killed, leaving the gardener with biologically "dead" garden soil with all the same problems of regular soil-poor drainage and sticky!

I'm banned from putting soil in the oven. That's OK...as you'll read in our section on harvest tips, I am allowed carrots in the washing machine.

STARTING SEEDS INDOORS

Top 3 Sensible Seed-Starting Tips

1. Good light is the secret to good seedlings.

2. Speed up germination with heat.

3. Water gently.

Supplies: Soil

Soil(Less) Mixes

The medium—the "soil"—we use for starting seeds indoors is frequently soilless. Here's why:

1. From the time a seed germinates until the arrival of "true leaves" (the first leaves are called seedling leaves), the young plant is nourished by nutrients in the seed. That means seeds don't need a nutrient-rich medium to germinate.

2. Garden soil packs down, making root growth more difficult, and limiting the entry of air into the soil. It is difficult to separate seedlings for transplanting out of hard-packed natural soil.

3. Unless you bake it in your oven, garden soil is not sterile. Sterility doesn't matter in the garden, but when you're starting your season's worth of crops indoors, it sure does.

Many commercial soilless mixes contain varying combinations of peat moss, perlite, vermiculite, ground limestone, and nutrients. They are generally free from weed seeds, harmful bacteria, and fungal diseases—and have a light texture that allows movement of air and water. The sterile nature of such mixes is particularly important for gardeners who decide not to use treated seeds, as it minimizes the risk of fungal diseases, collectively called "damping off."

It's buyer beware when it comes to potting soil and soilless mixes: there's a lot of crap on the market. We wouldn't waste our time and seeds with anything less than a professional soil mix.

Not sure how to read the label? Here are some tips:

✳ Avoid anything that promises slow- or timed-release fertilizer. Some granular fertilizers can release in bursts. While not a problem for larger plants, a burst of fertilizer could spell the demise of a tender seedling—killing it with too much food.

✳ If the label says humus, but no more, be suspicious about what sort of humus you're getting: is it composted bark, cow manure, or municipal waste?

✳ Is the mix sterile? If it contains topsoil and doesn't specify that it's been sterilized, be suspicious!

Soilless Mixes And Seeding

We recommend using commercially prepared soilless mix when first starting seeds because it is easy to use for beginners and practical for experienced gardeners.

There are soilless mixes made especially for seeding. A key feature is usually that everything is more finely milled—just as baby food is pureed.

 She said

I like to use a specialty seeding mix. It is good for small containers and really good in seedling trays with small openings, where one clump of mix could bung up an entire planting hole. I suggest newbies use the types of soilless mix

A LOOK AT COMMON SOILLESS MIX INGREDIENTS

INGREDIENT	ABOUT
Coir	Derived from coconut husks, often sold as an alternative to peat moss. Holds a lot of water, which can leave small seedlings waterlogged.
Compost	Various qualities available. Can add beneficial (and not-so-beneficial) microbes to a mix. A source of nutrients. Not sterile.
Perlite	Thermally expanded volcanic rock that is porous. Contains no nutrients. Doesn't hold water. Sterile. Lightweight.
Sand	Used to improve drainage and aeration—and add weight. Not necessarily sterile, unless it's been sterilized.
Sphagnum Peat Moss	Partially decomposed sphagnum moss, a plant that grows in bogs. Holds a lot of water when moistened (but repels it when dry). No nutritional value. Too acidic for many microbes, which is good for disease prevention.
Vermiculite	Thermally expanded mica-like material that is porous, lightweight, and sterile. Also used as insulation. Unlike perlite, it holds moisture and nutrients.
Worm Castings	This is the fancy term for worm droppings—otherwise known as worm poo. They add both nutrients and microbes (which continue to release nutrients into a soil mix). Not sterile.

...sold as "seed-starting blend" or "Ideal for seed starting." These mixes are generally a finer grade and do not have a built-in fertilizer charge.

He said Nice, but not necessary: It's an added expense and something else to store. If you plant enough seed, it doesn't matter if one or two seeds have their passage blocked by hulking chunks of a coarser soil mix.

She said A homemade mix or no-name mix that's too sweet or sour can cause weird problems. I've seen aluminum toxicity in plants grown in acidic potting mixes. By the time you see the problem, you have wasted your seed and soil and perhaps the whole season.

Supplies: Containers

Scour The Recycling Bin

While we recommend new gardeners start with commercially prepared soilless mixes for starting seeds, we don't recommend the same for containers. Be creative and don't feel you have to buy the combo packs of trays, cell packs, and clear covers that are stocked by garden centres. They're nice, but unnecessary.

Here are household items that you can use to start seeds:

- Toilet-paper rolls snipped in two, giving small pots.
- Cardboard pint and half-pint containers used to sell fruit.
- Cardboard tissue boxes with the top cut off.
- Plastic trays and foam trays in which produce is sold (if at least a couple of inches deep).
- Newspaper rolled into small pots. Visit www.GardenCoachesChat.com for instructions.
- Yogurt and margarine tubs with holes poked in the bottom.
- Old cell packs. (The plastic four- and six-pack squares in which annual bedding plants are sold.)

She said Personally, I am not starting seed in toilet paper rolls!

He said I don't use egg cartons because I find they're too shallow.

She said I wash the seeding trays and any pots over 10 cm (four inches) in width with soap and water. I don't own any bleach. Maybe I have been lucky.

He said I started buying bleach again when, one year, I lost half of my crop of seedlings to damping off.

She said I like seeding trays because they give me space for many kinds of seeds all at once—in a small area. For later transplanting, I like root-trainers—extra deep cells that are good for long-rooted plants or those that dislike being disturbed. They encourage deeper rooting than cell packs but take up less growing space for the same number of plants.

DON'T GIVE YOUR SEEDLINGS THE COOTIES

When reusing pots, cell packs, and trays, it's extremely important to sterilize them with a 10 per cent bleach solution. That's because they may harbour "damping off" disease, which will become active as seedlings start growing.

* Scrub off any old soil clinging to the sides.

* Mix 1 part bleach with 9 parts water.

* Soak for 15 minutes.

* Allow to air dry.

When using new containers for the first time or items from the recycling bin, you probably don't need to sterilize as there is unlikely to be any damping off disease present.

Buying Seeding Containers

If you want to buy supplies rather than recycling household "stuff" there are lots of models of "seeding trays" on the market alongside the more traditional cell packs and trays.

He said Every year I reuse cell packs in which annual bedding plants are sold. And when I run out of those I'll use pots or other containers—and start scavenging the recycling bin. The seedling trays and root-trainers are nice...but I don't want to fork out the money for them. (Admission: when shopping with Donna this past year, I bought a few for trials.)

She said Individual seeding trays or trays with section dividers prevent damping off disease from spreading beyond the affected container or row.

He said One spring when I was a kid, Dido stayed for a few weeks with us in Toronto. He helped me plant and grow yellow tomato seeds—which I chose because of the novel colour. When we returned home from the garden centre, supplies were scant. There was potting soil, but no plastic flats, no cell packs, no labels—and certainly no seeding gadgetry. He fetched a plastic washbasin from the laundry room, added a few

From top: small tomato seedling in a pot; a seeding tray with separate rows.

handfuls of potting soil, tore open the seed packet, casually sprinkled on some seeds, and then had me sprinkle on some more. We covered them with a bit of soil and were done, except for a label made from masking tape.

Supplies: Calendar

One of the most important items in the seeding toolkit is the calendar. Try a two-pronged approach to remembering seeding dates:

❀ Find seeding dates on seed packets or calculate them yourself, then mark them on your calendar;

❀ Sort your seed packets by planting date. Everything you plan to plant at a given number of weeks before the last spring frost should be grouped together.

She said I write the date I plan to start the seeds on each seed packet, but try to group things into two to three planting dates to keep things simple.

Seeds and labels go into trays together. (Note: tomato seeds are not naturally coloured: these are coloured so gardeners can easily distinguish between varieties.)

Supplies: All the Other Stuff

Transplanting
When it comes time to thin and transplant, a wooden Popsicle stick or an old fork are useful for digging and transporting seedlings to a new home.

She said I use a wooden pencil for transplanting because it is narrow and my husband loves Sudoku, so there's a good supply of pencils on hand.

Labels
Instead of commercially available labels, masking tape works well on pots. And plastic yogurt containers can be cut into strips to make labels, on which a permanent marker can be used.

He said My friend Cliff introduced me to an inexpensive label: wooden tongue depressors used by doctors.

Peas

I ♥ SUDOKU

Heirloom Tomatoes
Rainbow's End

"Set a table in the garden"
—Renee Shepherd

Zebra

Brandywine

MARVEL STRIPE

You don't have to steal them from the doctor: Just visit a medical supply store.

She said I label everything, and once used old mini-venetian blinds cut into strips. When I ran out of blinds, I switched to waxed milk cartons for labels. I always use pencil because "permanent" markers fade in the sun.

Lights And Timers

Many people think you need special bulbs to provide seedlings a complete spectrum. You don't need them. Two cool fluorescent tubes are sufficient. If you're buying or making a light stand, an important feature is to be able to lower and raise lights so they are 15–20 cm (6–8 inches) above seedlings.

Unless you have a fabulous memory and are always at home, hook your lights up to a timer to make sure your seedlings get enough light (see "Let's Simplify Light" on page 84). You might also consider using a fan if the growing area is warm, as air movement promotes stockier plants.

He said Do two fluorescent tubes give ideal light? No. But it's not a problem because we're growing indoors for a short time, then moving the transplants to the garden. Who cares if they're perfect?

She said If you are growing seedlings indoors until they reach flowering size (as I sometimes do with tomato plants) consider adding one warm fluorescent tube for each cool one used.

81

All about Timing

Timing of seed starting is often a confusing thing for new gardeners, as not all books and seed packets say the same thing.

The confusion is made worse by the fact that planting dates are linked to the last spring frost date...something that varies by region. Think of that date as a beacon that guides you to an appropriate planting date. Simply work backwards from the average last spring frost date.

Visit www.GardenCoachesChat.com to look for frost dates in your area.

When plants reach transplanting size too soon before they can go in the garden, they become root-bound, will wilt easily, and quickly use up the food in the soil. That's stressful for the plants—and plants that undergo such stress won't always recover once planted in the garden.

When to Start Seeds Indoors

WEEKS before last Spring frost CROPS

Weeks	Crops
10–12	celery, eggplant, leeks, onions, parsley, peppers
6–8	basil, early lettuce, okra, tomatoes
6	broccoli, Brussels sprouts, cabbage, cauliflower, kohlrabi
4	cucumber, lettuce (once again), melons, pumpkins, squash

Not all vegetables are started indoors: beans, beets, carrots, parsnip, peas, radish, and spinach are examples of crops that are sown directly in the garden.

Others, such as cucumbers or lettuce, can be started indoors for an early crop, and then sown directly in the garden for a later crop.

She said A word of caution: cauliflower and related crops, such as broccoli and cabbage, when started in warm indoor conditions then moved into cooler outdoor conditions, may get all mixed up and try to flower too soon. It's called "bolting"...and that's a problem because the crop will go to seed even before it forms a nice plant.

Heat mats speed germination.

SMART CHOICES FOR TRAY MATES

She said Some years I have combined the wrong seeds in seeding trays. Lettuce, for instance, is up in as little as two days while parsley might take a month. Because I want to uncover the seeds once they are up, this staggered germination complicates things. Think about speed of germination when choosing tray mates for your plants.

RELAX ABOUT TIMING

Timing is not a precise science. Off by a week? It probably doesn't make a huge difference to your crop. Luckily, it's usually better to start too late than too early.

CHECKING SEED VIABILITY

If you have old seed and aren't sure if it's still viable, put a dozen seeds on a moist paper towel within a clear sandwich bag, then watch how many seeds germinate.

Seeding Methods

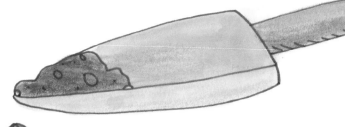

Let's oversimplify planting for a second: all we're doing is providing the seeds a moist, warm environment that will encourage germination. Some gardeners turbo-charge the germination process by pre-soaking seeds in warm water for 24 hours.

It's easy for people with small, home gardens to grow more seedlings indoors than needed. Resist the urge to plant too many—it just means more thinning later.

SEEDING METHOD

Choose Soil(less) Mix	Choose it carefully!
Moisten the Soil Mix	Soilless mixes are dry or only marginally moistened. It's extremely important to wet the soil before you plant. Dry peat moss repels water, and it's very difficult to wet it afterwards. Simply put the mix in a tub or pail, add some warm water, and mix with your hands. You want the mix to be moist, not sopping wet so that it drips when you squeeze a handful. Think of fluffy chocolate cake.
Choose a Container	Some crops transplant well, some don't. For example, tomatoes transplant without resentment and, where space is an issue, can be started in a flat or tiny individually seeded cells.
Add Soil to Container	Next, fill the container with soilless mix. *Don't bother tamping, which many books recommend as a way to remove air pockets. Instead, simply tap the filled container on the bench or the ground. The soilless mix will sink a bit, leaving you room to add your seeds and some more mix.*
Seeds Meet Soil	When seeding, you want enough space so seedlings will not crowd each other out before it's time to transplant (either into a larger container indoors or the final destination outdoors). We're simply putting our seeds atop the soil in our containers. If you're worried that we're now up to the top of the container, don't be. As we water, it will compress. ✽ Hand sprinkle (broadcast) the seeds from the packet onto the soil. Sometimes tapping seed packets will dispense the seed uniformly. But not always. ✽ If it's not working, try this: For small seed, it often helps to use a piece of folded paper, dump the seeds into the fold and tap or use something with points (a finishing nail works well) to measure out seed. Next, cover the seeds by adding a thin layer of soilless mix over top (2–3 times the diameter of the seed). Now tap the container again to remove air pockets. What about very fine seeds, such as celery and oregano? It's hard to put 2–3 times the seed diameter of soil over such small seeds. To make things simple, forget about adding soil—just lightly press seed into the soil surface. *Instead of using soil mix to cover the seeds, some gardeners will use fine vermiculite or sand. The idea is that a fine, lumpless covering makes it easier for seedlings to poke through. I don't bother.*

Continued on next page

Water and Cover

There are two ways to water:

✻ Use a watering can (gently, so as not to wash away soil).

✻ From the bottom by setting the tray or plant pots in water.

Don't bother with the advice of many books, which preach strict bottom watering. Use a watering can and water slowly to keep things simple.

My friend Melaine uses a spray bottle to water newly planted seeds.

Now that everything is planted and watered, we cover it to keep it moist. This is where we use a plastic dome or clear plastic bag.

Place on a warm surface if available. (On top of a hot water radiator works well, or use a commercially available heat mat.)

Check daily for moisture and for germination. **BE PATIENT**. Germination takes anywhere from a couple of days to almost a month, depending on the crop and on the growing conditions. You likely won't have to water often (or at all) with your seeds covered.

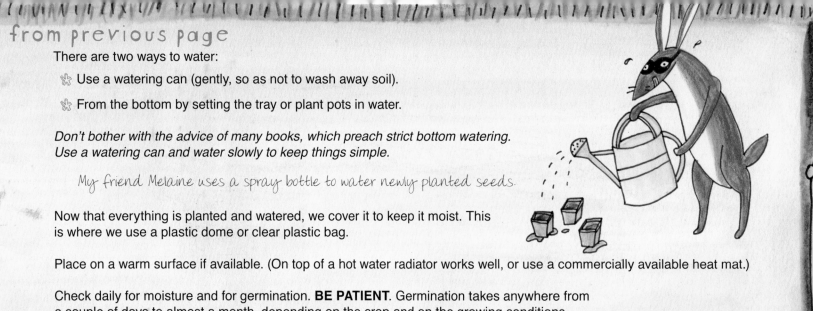

LARGE SEEDS

Larger seeds—such as cucumber, okra, and squash—are often planted in groups of two or three to a pot. Simply poke a hole with a finger or a pencil, and then drop in the seed. There is no need to use special fine seedling mix.

When you're dealing `She said` *with small quantities of large seeds, such as cucumber, you can pre-soak them in a damp paper towel within a plastic bag. Then, move the individual seedlings to their own pots as soon as they sprout.*

`He said` Sounds practical, Donna, but for me, it's too much of a bother to pre-soak seeds. They'll come up when they're ready.

Visit www.GardenCoachesChat.com to see our video about starting seeds.

Growing Conditions

Let's Simplify Light

Some seeds need light to germinate, while others prefer darkness for germination. This often has gardeners thinking about how much soil to put over seeds—and where to place seeds to allow for or exclude light.

Let's cut to the chase: it really doesn't make a difference with most vegetables. Some authorities recommend light for lettuce. Other than that, forget about light for germination. Put seed trays in a warm dark spot. Light becomes important once the seeds have germinated.

There is nothing more low-input than growing seedlings on a windowsill. But for gardeners who don't have a bright windowsill—or who grow more seedlings than the windowsill can accommodate—artificial lighting is necessary. Bright light is important because it promotes compact growth and ordinary cool florescent bulbs work fine for seedlings.

If the height of the lights cannot be adjusted, use boxes under the plants to bring the plants closer to the lights. Give plants under lights 12–16 hours of artificial light per day.

Let's Simplify Temperature

Temperature is one of those factors that can overwhelm new gardeners. With different optimal temperatures for seed germination and plant growth, and different optimal temperatures for different species, many people worry about how to cater to all their seedlings.

BEFORE GERMINATION	AFTER GERMINATION
In most cases, you want seeds at or warmer than room temperature for germination.	After germination, seedlings are best grown somewhere cooler than room temperature, as this promotes sturdy growth.
Putting this into practical application, it means that newly planted seeds can be placed in warm areas, such as above a fridge. There are commercial water-resistant heat mats available that are designed for starting seeds and growing heat-loving plants.	Cool temperatures for growing seedlings are ideal but the ballasts from the florescent lights often mean the air above the plants gets warm. Keeping the air moving can counteract the heat and make seedlings stronger—this can be achieved quite simply with a fan.
Remember that a windowsill may not have ideal temperatures for germination: While it can be warm during the day, it can become quite cool at night.	

He said · I found that the best warm spot for germinating in my previous house was in the basement, on a shelf near the ceiling and beside a heat duct. It was ideal. Unfortunately, I moved...so have started using a heat mat.

She said · I have a heated floor in my basement and have had overnight germination of the quickest growing plants such as lettuce!

Let's Simplify Humidity And Air Movement

BEFORE GERMINATION	AFTER GERMINATION
High humidity is generally good for germinating seeds. That's why gardeners make a microclimate with a clear plastic dome that covers the seeding tray, or with a clear plastic bag.	Once seedlings are up, it's time to remove the covering. The reason is that, once sprouted, your seedlings no longer require such high moisture levels—which also happen to be ideal for disease.
	Use a misting bottle to elevate humidity once the cover is removed.
	If plants are near a window, keep the window open when the weather is fine.

She said · When I use clear plastic bags, the humidity builds, and the bags stick to my seedlings! I buy the clear domes.

A plastic dome keeps humidity high until seeds sprout.

He said · I find the domes are a worthwhile purchase too—and have had some last at least a dozen years.

She said · I use new bottles for misting because I am concerned about contaminants in bottles from previous contents. It probably sounds like I am shopping constantly, but once I buy a bottle I use it for years.

He said · I don't mist my seedlings.

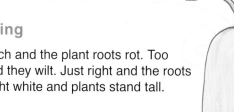

Watering

Too much and the plant roots rot. Too little and they wilt. Just right and the roots are bright white and plants stand tall.

Different containers need more or less water depending on container size and location—if a plant is close to the window or fan, it will dry out more quickly.

GROWING CONDITIONS Not Perfect?

Here's the key thing to remember about growing conditions: even if you don't have the perfect conditions, don't despair. Chances are that you can still grow decent transplants—even if they don't look quite as good as the ones for sale in the store.

From top: healthy tomato seedling; crowded seedlings; tomato seedlings transplanted deeper; lettuce tolerates seeding into open flats.

Believe It Or Not... T.L.C.

Donna likes to touch her plants. She will daily run her hand over germinated seedlings and young plants. This is really more than simple affection though: The action of brushing the plants promotes stockier growth.

A small fan on seedlings for a couple of hours each day has a similar effect.

He said Donna, you obviously don't have little kids. There's no way I could find the time to do that!

On The Operating Table: Pricking Out

The term "pricking out" is often used to refer to the process of separating and replanting seedlings grown together in a flat or a pot.

Have you ever tried to shimmy your way to a bright window seat on a crowded bus, where you barely have space to stand and the person next to you keeps stepping on your toes? If so, then you can guess what it's like for seedlings to reach for the light in a crowded pot. And that's why we thin and repot seedlings.

Thinning breaks the heart of many new and seasoned gardeners alike. Having nurtured a seed from germination, it seems counterintuitive to take out a tender young seedling and leave it to die. But to be kind, you must be cruel. Just think of that crowded bus and remember that too many seedlings in a pot will give you spindly, weak plants.

The reason for crowding is simple: It's rare that 100 per cent of seeds will germinate. So we always put in a few extra seeds. For example, if we're using a pot for a single cucumber plant, it makes sense to start with two or three seeds. Once they're up, we can choose the best and thin out the rest. Cucumbers don't like to be transplanted so instead of separating out the plants, we just thin the extras by cutting them off at the base.

86

Pricking Out and Transplanting Guidelines

1. See if your seedlings are big enough to transplant. After the first two "seedling" leaves grow, they are followed by "true" leaves. Prick out seedlings once they have two true leaves.

2. Prepare new containers for planting (so that seedling roots are exposed to air for the shortest time possible).

3. Make labels and put them in trays.

4. In the newly filled and labelled container, poke a hole into the soil with a dibbler. (OK, we're being show-offs with lingo: this is just a pointed implement that could be a pencil or Popsicle stick.)

5. Remove a seedling from its crowded home using the dibbler.

6. Hold the seedling by the leaves, not the stem. Tender stems can easily crush, and the plant will never recover, while it can always grow a new leaf.

7. Get as much soil with the roots as possible, then transport this on your hand, an old fork, or a Popsicle stick.

8. Plop the seedling into the hole you made in step 2.

9. You want the plant to be at the same depth as it was previously (except for tomatoes, which can be planted more deeply).

10. Firm the soil lightly around the stem using index fingers and thumbs.

11. Water immediately.

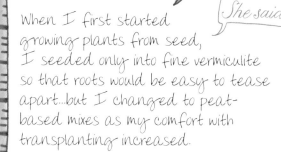

She said

When I first started growing plants from seed, I seeded only into fine vermiculite so that roots would be easy to tease apart...but I changed to peat-based mixes as my comfort with transplanting increased.

If your space is unlimited and friends are lining up around the block for your plants, go ahead and transplant every seed that germinates. Otherwise, if 175 tomato seeds germinate and the garden can only hold 10 plants, thin and only transplant the best plants. (But leave the others in the seeding tray until you are sure the ones you moved have survived.)

Separation Anxiety?

If the thought of teasing apart clumps of seedlings for transplanting is daunting, try this: sow two to three seeds into their own small pot, where they can stay until it is time to go outdoors or to a bigger pot. This takes a lot more room initially but might be a good way to ease into the whole starting-from-seed thing. This is also a good tactic for plants that spend a short stint inside, such as squash, melons, and cucumbers (which we only seed four weeks before the last frost).

If you have accidentally planted too many seeds, use scissors to clip and remove the extras so that the ones remaining have the best chance and are not forced to grow on in a crowded situation. (If you yank them out, you could pull out the strong seedling as well.)

He said I like to grow lots of tomato plants—and my thinning and repotting techniques vary, depending on how many plants of a given variety I require.

With some varieties, I only want a couple of plants. That was the case with the yellow cherry tomato plants I grew with my kids this year. They helped me sow a few seeds in a couple of pots. Once the seeds were up, we thinned (using scissors) until there was just one plant remaining in each pot.

With favourite varieties, though, I want a lot of plants. If I started all of those seeds in their own pots, it would take up far too much space in my warm germinating area. So I plant the seeds together in one pot. Once they're up and have true leaves, I prick them out and replant each into its own pot.

88

MYCORRHIZAE FOR SEEDS AND SEEDLINGS

In a mycorrhizal relationship, a mycorrhizal fungus colonizes plant roots. The fungus gets carbohydrates from the plant, while the plant gets water and minerals from the fungus. Most plants have some sort of mycorrhizal relationship—and garden centres now sell commercially prepared mycorrhizae. Some vegetables, though, such as the cabbage and beet families, don't co-operate with mycorrhizae.

Seeds can be mixed with the powder prior to planting, or transplant roots can be dipped into it while repotting.

He said The science behind supplemental mycorrhizae makes sense: boost levels of naturally occurring fungi to give plants a head start. But to me, it's an unnecessary input. Think of the human diet: we can gorge on supplements such as vitamins and omega-3 extracts...or we can eat fresh fruit and vegetables and food containing things our bodies need. Feed your plants with healthy garden soil—forget all the commercial inputs.

She said I use mycorrhizae, but not consistently or continuously: just when I feel like it.

Rx
Prescription For Seedling Care

Rx from the Coaches' Dispensary

www.GardenCoachesChat.com

Toronto and Calgary

Dispense as written. No substitutions.

LIQUIDS

Moist soil only. If soil gets soggy or dry, pay more attention.

MEALS

Modest amounts of nutrients only. Overfeeding will hamper treatment.

REST

Give about 12 hours of rest daily… YES that means about 12 hours of light if using artificial light.

FRESH AIR

Where air is stagnant, consider a fan to keep air moving.

OTHER SYMPTOMS

Lanky growth may indicate excessive heat.

Take prescription daily until plants are in tip-top shape.

Post-Op Care: Watering Transplanted Seedlings

Experienced greenhouse growers never let new staff do the watering because this is actually trickier than it looks! Add a small amount of water at first transplant, just enough so that it runs out the bottom.

Check daily, but only water when the soil surface is starting to dry and the container, when picked up, feels lighter. Newly transplanted seedlings may not need extra water for four or five days after the first watering, but as they get bigger, they need more. Eventually plants need watering daily, and then they either need to be moved up to a bigger size of pot or, if the weather conditions are right, the plant can be moved outdoors.

He said Remember that when watering from above, you can topple your young seedlings. To avoid this, try not to hit your seedlings with the stream of water, especially with very small seedlings.

URP

She said The other important point to mention about watering is the quality. It's best if it's not too icy cold or full of chlorine, so leave water sitting overnight to warm and off-gas the chlorine.

Rain barrel water may seem ideal but it is hard to say if there are impurities from roof or rain. Small seedlings are very susceptible to all kinds of trouble so use tap water until plants move outdoors.

He said You mean you don't have a water-warming gadget?

He said All these years later, I can still picture the wilted, dead-looking tomato seedlings on the patio—the same seedlings that Dido helped me plant. I hate to admit it... but I think I cried. In his gruff way, he shrugged off the disaster, soaked them with water, and told me not to worry. They bounced right back. Lesson: seedlings are not always as delicate as they look.

Post-Op Care: Feeding Transplanted Seedlings

Seeds contain enough nutrients to nourish the germinating seedling. By the time true leaves arrive, though, it's time to think about minerals the plants will need.

The important thing to remember about feeding is that you can quickly harm your seedlings by overfeeding. The sensitive, young roots burn easily—by natural and synthetic fertilizers alike. Small seedlings need nutrients in small quantities.

She said We often use the words "food" or "feeding" but of course the miracle of plants is that they make their own food from the sun. All we really need to give plants are the building blocks: oxygen, carbon, and minerals.

I transplant into a commercially purchased media with added worm castings (which contribute microbes and nutrition). Numerous studies I've read over the years repeat that 5-10 per cent by volume of castings to soil mix is ideal, so I stick to that ratio and only rarely feed my seedlings with additional fertilizers.

If you are using fertilizers, and the label does not recommend a dilution rate for seedlings, the rate for indoor or potted plants is likely fine. If in doubt, cut the rate in half. Too little is better than too much.

Most soilless mixes contain a small amount of "food," often called a "charge." It's no substitute for feeding. A compost- or soil-based mix, on the other hand, may have sufficient nutrients to nurture the seedlings until it's time to put them in the garden, especially for crops such as cucumbers that are only in the container for a short while.

She said Many people ask if you can grow seedlings in pure compost. No.
If you know you have a great compost you can add it to your soil mix for larger plants—but don't use it for seedlings because they are so sensitive to salts in compost.

He said I rely on compost and microbes once my seedlings are in the garden soil—but while they're in that unnatural environment of a plastic pot, soilless mix, and fluorescent light, I feed them with fertilizer, albeit very low doses and far less frequently than prescribed. That's why my seedlings are sometimes a bit yellow and underfed when I put them in the ground.

SEEDLING FERTILIZER SHOPPING
Lingo

Confused by numbers, formulations, and lingo? Here is more information to help you shop for seedling food:

ORGANIC
As we explained earlier, in a scientific sense, organic means that it contains carbon.

But certified organic may also mean that the product has been approved for use in organic production.

NATURAL
May describe products from "natural" sources, e.g. manure.

Natural does not equal safe.

INORGANIC | SYNTHETIC | CONVENTIONAL
These three terms are often used interchangeably to describe fertilizer that is not organic.

The irony here is that the term conventional—which is especially common in agricultural circles—describes fertilizers that are relatively new on the scene. Manure was the conventional choice for millennia.

Water Soluble or Granular
❋ Use a water-soluble (not granular) product because a granule touching a seedling could spell its demise.

❋ Picture a granule spewing vast quantities of food all over a tender seedling root…and you'll understand why.

Those Numbers…
❋ Fertilizer labels have three bold numbers on every label, which represents the percentages of nitrogen, phosphorus, and potassium (N-P-K).

❋ The lower the number, the smaller the percentage of N or P or K.

❋ Read the whole label—not just the three big numbers. If the label says the product contains trace elements (also known as micronutrients), that's good.

❋ Look for balanced numbers. Organic products are usually bulkier, so have lower numbers (e.g. 2-2-2) than inorganic products (e.g. 20-20-20).

She said my concern with all fertilizers is that "filler" ingredients are not explained or listed on the label. This may not be a concern if the product is certified organic, but in other cases what is it and why won't companies tell us?

He said My fertilizer of choice for indoor seedlings is a water-soluble inorganic fertilizer. It's locally made, minimally packaged, and economical—and has a full diet of trace elements.

Pests and Diseases

She said Transplants from the store often come with their own baggage. The year I bought tomato transplants by mail order, I got a free bonus: bugs that attacked my homegrown transplants.

Damping Off

The main disease that affects seedlings is damping off. This is actually not only one disease, but a few. Regardless of the responsible party, damping off makes seedlings suddenly topple, like trees felled in the forest by a lumberjack. The stems are girdled by dying tissue, and they simply fall over.

Checklist to Prevent Damping Off

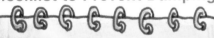

- Sterilize containers and seeding supplies.

- Avoid excessive humidity or overwatering once seeds have germinated.

- Use sterile potting mixes such as peat-based mixes.

- Avoid bargain potting mixes…which often either contain the disease or provide lousy drainage that encourages disease.

Fungus Gnats

Fungus gnats are small black insects often seen flying around seedlings. They often arrive as eggs in poor quality seeding mixes. The flying adults don't trouble the seedlings: it's the small worm-like larvae in the soil, which munch on seedling roots. The larvae like damp conditions—so avoiding overwatering is one step in preventing a population explosion.

She said I use microscopic worms called nematodes—bought from a mail-order supplier—for fungus gnat control in both plants and in my worm bin. Nematodes are aggressive attackers of both fungus gnat larvae and fruit fly larvae that would otherwise multiply astronomically in my worm bin.

Indoor Seeding Guff Busted

Guff Says

When growing seedlings, coir-based soilless mixes are best for the environment.

GUFFAWERS RESPOND

We often hear that coir (which comes from coconut husks) is the green alternative to peat moss, which comes from peat bogs.

Coconut plantations are far from environmentally inert—and may be growing on land that was formerly rainforest. Add to that the fact that coir must be transported around the world to reach North American gardeners, and we don't buy the argument. It all sounds pretty energy-intensive for an inferior imported product that replaces a product made by North American workers.

Like the gravel and aggregates used to build our roads, peat moss is "mined." Use peat moss judiciously, where it offers true benefits, such as starting seeds. If you're amending garden soil, it's unnecessary, so use compost instead.

Interested in a homegrown, sustainable peat replacement? Bark is a by-product of the forestry industry. There are some bark-peat growing mixes on the market now—and we would not be surprised to see more in the future.

Guff Says

All worm castings are created equal.

GUFFAWERS RESPOND

Worm castings are easy to make at home, but they are commercially available too. If you buy castings to add to your soilless mix, consider this: what goes in greatly affects what comes out.

Some commercial worm growers feed worms peat instead of plant waste or manure. This leaves the green consumer with a couple of things to ponder:

- ❧ Is it environmentally wise to feed worms carbon that has been taken from long-term storage (peat) when plant residues and manure (carbon not locked into long-term storage) work well?

- ❧ How will the microbial makeup of the castings differ for worms on such a boring diet?

She said If you are buying castings, ask the supplier if the product has been tested for good biology. Better still, start raising your own worms, feed them a varied diet, and use your own castings.

Guff Says

Peat pots are better than plastic ones because they decompose.

GUFFAWERS RESPOND

Both peat and manure pots act like wicks, rapidly drawing moisture out of the soil and away from seedlings. For a busy gardener, that means seedlings dried beyond recognition. If you decide to use them, make sure that none of the wick-like pot is exposed above the soil when planting outdoors.

She said I received cow-manure pots as a trial one year, and they were a disaster.

Guff Says

The earlier you start seeds indoors, the bigger the transplants and the earlier the harvest.

GUFFAWERS RESPOND

Ever heard of too much of a good thing? Members of the cabbage family actually go downhill quickly if left too long in warm indoor conditions. If in doubt, always double check how much time you should give the seeds before planting out. Start your broccoli or cauliflower or cabbage no more than six to seven weeks before your last spring frost.

For example: If your last frost is on June 1, start the seeds of the cabbage family no sooner than mid-April. If your last frost is in mid-April, start the seeds at the beginning of March. Even though you start later in cooler northern climates, plants will grow faster because the days are longer. If experience tells you there is not enough time for a crop to mature (because of a very short frost-free period) then provide plants with outdoor shelter in the spring and fall to extend the growing season. (See "Make Your Own Crop-Boosting Microclimate" on page 17.)

She said There are exceptions: some plants, such as tomatoes, are usually started about 10 weeks before the last frost but they have more tolerance for indoor growth and can be started as early as 20 weeks before planting outside if, and only if, there is space to keep moving plants up into bigger pots as they grow. If started in January, they will be in five gallon pots and probably already have fruit by outdoor planting time in June or July.

Guff Says

All soilless mixes are basically the same.

GUFFAWERS REPLY

Some have high quality peat, and some don't. The top of a peat bog gives a lighter coloured peat with long fibres that permit better air movement—and less chance of drowned seedlings. Dark peat from the bottom of the bog (often sold as garden peat) has short fibres and is not as good for soilless growing mixes.

Some mixes contain improperly composted materials, giving elevated levels of compounds that can harm plants. Other mixes do not have the correct air-to-soil balance, so the mix becomes compacted and water does not drain away, leaving seedling roots to rot. Still other mixes have high levels of salts. It pays to shop around.

Indoor Seeding Q&A

My pepper seeds didn't germinate, but my other seeds did. Why?

She said Commercial growers know peppers are the trickiest plants to grow and are very subject to microbial, environmental, and soil factors. Keep seedling trays warm by providing bottom heat. Once seeds are up, keep the light bright and run a fan at least a few hours a day to keep the humidity lower and air circulating. In other words, treat your peppers like the queens they are.

He said Check whether the seeds are old. While pepper seeds can last for a few years, your success with fresh seed will be better. Don't buy seed packets that are dusty—and remember to date envelopes containing seed you save yourself.

Real Vegetable Gardeners Don't...

Real vegetable gardeners don't become faint-hearted at the task of thinning.

Growing good seedlings requires giving them enough space. And that often means thinning.

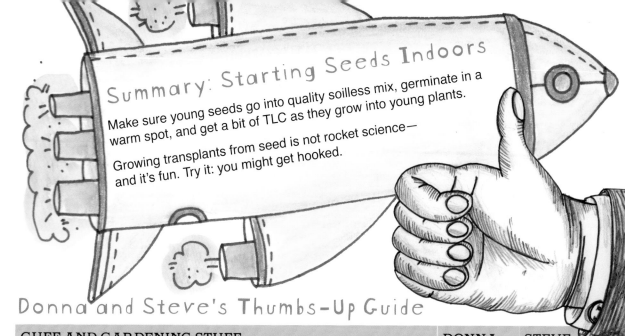

Summary: Starting Seeds Indoors

Make sure young seeds go into quality soilless mix, germinate in a warm spot, and get a bit of TLC as they grow into young plants.

Growing transplants from seed is not rocket science—and it's fun. Try it: you might get hooked.

Donna and Steve's Thumbs-Up Guide

GUFF AND GARDENING STUFF		DONNA	STEVE
1. Climate	Row Covers	Up	Down
	Cold Frames	Up	Up
2. Soil	Rotating Composters	Up	Down
	Rototilling	Down	Up
3. Planning	Planning Perfectionism	Down	Down
	Flowers Mixed with Veg	Up	Up
4. Garden Making	Pythagorean Theorem	Up	Down
	Double Digging	Down	Down
5. Crop Selection	Broad Beans	Down	Up
	Asparagus Pea	Down	Down
	Rotation	Up	Down
6. Indoor Seeding	Peat-Based Soilless Mixes	Up	Up
	Fine Textured Seeding Mixes	Up	Down
	Coir-Based Mixes	Down	Down

Garden Coaches Chat: No guff. Lots of fun.
for more details visit www.GardenCoachesChat.com

OUTDOOR SEEDING & TRANSPLANTING

Top 3 Sensible Seeding and Transplanting Tips

1. Don't underplant: overplant.
2. Stagger seeding dates to push the seasons.
3. When transplanting, mind the stem: a squished stem is as good as gone.

Ready the Soil

What can we tell you about readying the soil for seeding and transplanting outdoors?

There are probably as many approaches as there are gardeners. But here's some of what you might do to ready the soil:

* Dig the soil lightly
* Break up clods
* Add compost
* Rake soil into beds

Steve likes to dig in the fall. Donna doesn't. Perfectionists may massage every last unsightly clump of soil from a bed with a rake, while others may not bother.

The key thing to remember is that when you're transplanting and have exposed roots at hand, having the soil ready for planting means less waiting time for the transplants.

Timing

Start Early with Volunteers

In farming lingo, the word volunteer describes crops that seed themselves. For farmers, volunteer crops can be weeds: volunteer corn is a weed in a soybean field. But in the home vegetable garden, volunteer crops give you an early start.

Let a few lettuce, spinach, or dill plants go to seed. Though the seeds scatter on their own, you can help spread them around the garden. They will be ready to germinate with the first rays of sunshine in the spring.

Start Early with Perennials

Perennials such as asparagus, chives, rhubarb, and sorrel give an early start in the vegetable garden.

She said I never actually grew sorrel before I met Steve, but now I am hooked!

He said If you intend to buy plants, wait until the spring rush is over. You'll find that retailers are often anxious to liquidate stock through the summer, so you can pick up these perennials at a good price.

Start Early with Plant Parts

You can grow onions from seed. But you can also buy what are called sets: small, cherry-sized onion bulbs that are planted in spring and mature into full-sized onions.

You can also buy a head of garlic and split it into individual cloves to plant in the fall, pointy side up. Like flowering daffodil bulbs, garlic must be planted early enough in fall to get established before winter, which gives plumper bulbs the next year.

Keep it simple: transplant chives as clumps of seedlings instead of individuals.

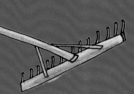

EYE ON POTATOES

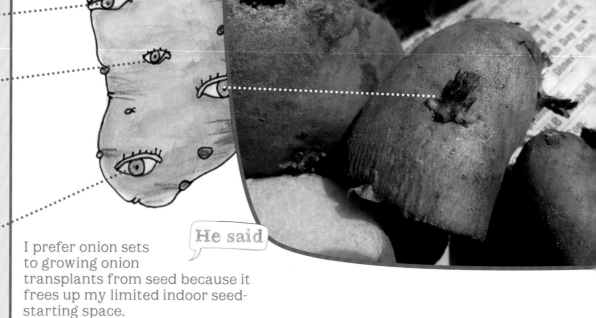

Potatoes aren't grown from seed. Instead, "seed" potatoes (potatoes saved from the previous year) are planted in the garden.

Seed potatoes can be planted whole, but the yield is greater if they are first cut into pieces. Figuring out where to cut is made easier by the fact that potatoes usually start to sprout in spring. Sprouts come from "eyes"—and every piece must have an eye. So a potato with ten eyes can give ten seed pieces to plant. Not bad!

Cut the potatoes in advance of planting. Some people cut and leave them in a dark paper bag. Donna cuts the potatoes and leaves the sections out in a cardboard box to air dry in the house. They can be pre-cut overnight or held for up to four days before planting.

Hold back some uncut potatoes in the fridge for a later crop. Mid-summer plantings produce baby potatoes in the fall, when the earlier plantings are already producing big mommas.

He said
I prefer onion sets to growing onion transplants from seed because it frees up my limited indoor seed-starting space.

She said
Specialty potato growers sell potatoes by the pound—which is great for home gardeners who don't need five or ten pounds of any one kind. If you haven't tried the Yellow Banana or Red Russian varieties, give them a try. Each potato has its own flavour and texture. All potatoes are not created equal.

He said
I haven't experimented a lot with potato varieties. I like Norland, a fairly common red-skinned variety with a white flesh. My kids love digging potatoes—it's like digging for pirate treasure.

Fall Seeding

You can seed crops such as dill, lettuce, and spinach in late summer or fall for a spring crop. That's part of the job of spring seeding taken care of...the year before!

Early Spring Seeding

Once the snow is off the ground and the soil thaws, you can start planting a lot of cold-hardy crops. These are crops that can germinate in cool temperatures and won't be injured by frost.

If you can work your soil (if it is neither frozen nor too "sticky"), the time to plant these cold-hardy crops has arrived. (See crops chart on page 68.)

Main Season Succession Planting

Fast finishers such as peas, radish, spinach, or lettuce can be planted early, then again as the summer progresses. In warmer climates, greens may be planted into early fall and—depending on the crop and the weather—harvested till the snow flies. In cooler climates, lettuce planted mid-summer may never fully mature—but, hey, it's like the small overpriced greens at the store.

Succession planting dates vary by climate—and microclimate. Use some of the tips from Chapter 1 to get more from your succession schemes as the weather cools in the fall.

Outdoor Seeding Methods

Drills

Most home gardens are too small for a commercial seeder or drill. If you want straight, long rows—and not everyone does—here's a practical approach:

❀ Tie a string to the ends of two strong stakes and place the stakes in the ground at the row ends.

❀ Drag a stick or hoe along the string through the garden to make a trench that is approximately 1 cm (½ inch) deep for big seeds such as beans, or just a scratch in the surface for small seeds such as carrots.

❀ Drop seeds in the trench at recommended spacing.

❀ If you are making wide rows instead of single rows, simply move the stakes over a few inches in the prepared soil then drill and seed the next row.

❀ Scatter soil, sand, or fine-screened compost to cover seed.

Scatter and Poke

Here's a great way for home gardeners to simplify planting peas and beans. It might make market gardeners chuckle, but it's actually quite practical in the home garden, where, instead of long, well-spaced rows planted for mechanical cultivation, we are dealing with small plots.

Steve's kids love this method, and can be heard repeatedly saying, "poke" as each seed goes in the ground.

❀ Scatter the seeds on the soil.

❀ Move them around until it looks as if there are approximately 10–15 cm (4–6 inches) between seeds.

❀ Then "poke" them into the earth with a finger, to a depth of 2–4 cm (1–2 inches).

❀ Scatter some soil to fill the holes.

He said Beet seeds are good candidates for this too, though they're a bit harder to see as they're dark like the soil.

Scatter

It's hard to see smaller seeds once scattered on the soil, let alone poke them in. Scattering and covering with soil results in a more random appearance than drilled rows, but is suited to growing in blocks and wide rows.

❀ Lightly scatter the seed over the prepared area.

❀ Lightly rake seed into place.

❀ Cover by scattering soil or screened compost. **He said**

She said Screening compost is for perfectionists.

Screening compost is fun and so rewarding.

SCREENING SOIL AND COMPOST

Screened compost or soil has simply had some of the coarser pieces removed, making it more suitable for seeds, which can be derailed by big clods in their path.

You can make a screen through which you "screen" soil and compost. Take one-quarter-inch wire mesh and affix it to a frame. (An old window or picture frame works well.) Rub the soil or compost over the mesh and catch whatever passes through below: that's your screened compost or soil.

Seed Spacing

Decrease Recommended Spacing

Seeds are cheap. Plant more seeds in a given space than suggested on the seed packet, anywhere from a quarter to a third more.

Recommended spacing is usually calculated to give picture-perfect vegetables and plants. But going for that perfect specimen often means sacrificing space in the garden—space that could support more vegetables. Think of it this way: planting vegetables more densely means more leaves to shade out competing weeds.

There's another reason too: denser planting means that with some crops you can start harvesting and eating sooner. Consider carrots: when planted too closely together they require thinning. As you thin them, you have baby carrots. Lettuce can also be thinned or moved around the garden as it sprouts and grows.

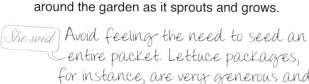 Avoid feeling the need to seed an entire packet. Lettuce packages, for instance, are very generous and contain enough seed for two or three seasons for most families, so only use a small portion at a time.

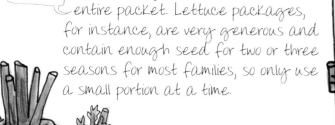

Watching for Germination

Once the garden has been seeded, the speed of germination will vary by plant and how warm the soil is in a given spot. Dark soil in raised beds will warm up more quickly than low-lying, heavy soil.

Some plants, such as lettuce, quickly poke up, while others, such as parsnip, take weeks to sprout.

He said I was set to contact the seed house to complain about the slow germination of my pea seeds one year. Then, when I inspected more closely, I found they were germinating well...but a rabbit was nibbling them off every morning before I came to the garden to check them.

When to Transplant Outside

WEEKS BEFORE LAST SPRING FROST

5–7	leeks, onions, parsley
3–4	bok choy, broccoli, cabbage, kale
2–3	lettuce
0	cauliflower, cucumber, summer squash, tomatoes

WEEKS AFTER LAST SPRING FROST

1–2	basil, eggplant, melons, peppers, pumpkins, squash

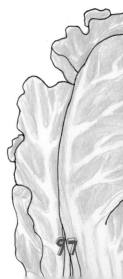

Tough Love ♥
Hardening Off

When it's almost time for your young plants to strike out on their own in the garden, it's time for tough love. And in gardening lingo, tough love is called "hardening off."

The indoor world of constant temperatures and fluorescent lights is no preparation for the real world outdoors. The goal of hardening off is to accustom your teenage plants to outdoor stresses such as wind, direct sunlight, drying soils, and temperature variations.

Here are some hardening-off measures:

♥ Withhold moisture. Water less but don't let plants wilt.

♥ Place outside in the shade for a couple days.

♥ Gradually place in sunlight, increasing the duration each day.

♥ Gradually expose plants to wind, rain, and sun. If there is a risk of overnight frost, bring them indoors.

♥ Transplant outside on a grey, rainy day, when the seedlings are less likely to dry out. Otherwise, plant late in the day to give the seedlings the benefit of cooler evening temperatures.

He said

I have tried to rush the hardening-off process on more than one occasion—and have had sunburnt tomato seedlings. It's not worth rushing.

How to Transplant Outdoors

❀ Water homegrown seedlings well. Water the plant in the morning if it is going in the ground that evening so the soil will stay together, and so the tender transplant is not off to a dry start.

❀ Ready the new home. Dig a hole into your well-prepared garden soil.

❀ Minimize root zone disturbance. With pots, invert and tap the bottom to coax out the plant. With cell packs, it's often easiest to push the bottom upwards with a finger and then gently grasp and pull out the plant.

❀ Place plant in the hole, without squeezing the stem.

❀ Fill the hole with soil. Tamp lightly with thumbs and first two fingers to ensure the root ball of the transplant is in contact with the surrounding soil.

❀ Water well afterwards.

❀ Keep tabs on your troops. If they look like they're suffering from too much sun, you can protect them with an inverted pot or row cover.

She said While in France, friends of mine saw leeks seeded thickly in an oak barrel in early spring. The farmer told them the leeks grow in the barrel all summer and are transplanted in late summer into rows in the garden-then harvested gradually over the winter. Most of us don't have the mild climate of France, but if you do, try this method.

IN THE TRENCHES: TOMATOES

There's a general rule in gardening, which is that whenever you transplant, you put the plant into the ground at the same depth it previously was. That's because most plants don't like a change in soil depth.

Tomatoes are an exception. That's good news because tomatoes get floppy if left in their pots too long or grown in less-than-ideal conditions. So if your tomato plants look floppy, bury them deeper than they were in the pot. Dig a trench, covering the stem with soil. The plant will form new roots where the stem is covered by soil.

VEGGIE GARDEN INSURANCE: SAVE EXTRA TRANSPLANTS

Hold back a few extra transplants. If there's a late frost, naughty cutworms, or marauding wildlife, you'll have something to replace transplants that succumb.

A Lifeline for Young Plants in Crisis

Sometimes unexpectedly cold spring weather can bring crisis to the veggie patch. Luckily, you can manipulate the temperature a bit even once your new transplants are in the ground—and throw them a lifeline.

If there is a risk of overnight frost once the plants are in the ground (and they're frost-sensitive), an inverted flowerpot placed over each plant is often enough to help them survive the night. For larger areas, a sheet of plastic or an old cotton sheet provides protection. The frost sits on the sheet instead of the plant. A row cover can also be used—and is suitable for covering a whole row of plants.

When They're Not Ready to Move Out

Sometimes, instead of a couple of frosty evenings, gardeners are challenged by a cold spring. Instead of rushing frost-tender plants into the ground, pot them into larger containers so they have room to keep growing until it is safe to put them into the ground.

She said I notice the local greenhouses sell tomatoes in five-gallon pots with small fruit already on them. This is how desperate we are for success in cool climates!

TRANSPLANTING AS A HARVEST-STAGGERING SHOCK TREATMENT

A full, perfect head of lettuce is a sight to behold…but often the perfection is short-lived, and gardeners are unable to eat the bounty before all the plants in the patch turn bitter and become unpalatable as they prepare to flower (bolt). If only there was a way to derail that instinct to flower…

Here's one way to make the lettuce plants act a bit cautiously and stay in the leafy stage longer: shock them by digging and transplanting them. The shock will often temporarily turn off the plant's readiness to bolt.

THOSE BRIGHT SUNNY DAYS…

Those bright sunny spring days bring out the transplanting itch in gardeners. But guess what? Those bright sunny days aren't the best time to transplant tender seedlings. An overcast day is better.

Outdoor Seeding and Transplanting Guff Busted

Guff Says

Be careful not to overplant the vegetable garden.

GUFFAWERS RESPOND

While it's true that growing too many plants in too small a space will reduce yield, don't forget:

- Some crops will grow well when seeded more densely than recommended.

- Not all seeds will germinate.

- For some crops, there's nothing wrong with too many seedlings: some you can transplant, while others you can thin out to eat.

Guff Says

All plants should go in the ground on the May 24 long weekend.

GUFFAWERS RESPOND

It's a Canadian tradition to plant the garden over the Victoria Day long weekend in May. But average last spring frost dates vary widely—and many of us can seed early crops well before the long weekend. Crops that can't tolerate frost should be seeded or transplanted well after May 24 in colder areas. (For average frost date data see www.GardenCoachesChat.com.)

She said In Calgary, gardeners often wait until after the last May or early June full moon to plant tender crops. With planning, organized gardeners in Victoria can grow cold-hardy vegetables year-round.

Guff Says

Transplants going into the garden require a transplant fertilizer.

GUFFAWERS RESPOND

No. Many soils have all the required nutrients. If the soil has a rich microbial mix, there will also be plenty of enzymes produced by fungi and bacteria to boost and stimulate new root growth.

She said In new gardens that are low in organic matter, or in soils where organic matter is depleted, or fertilizers and amendments have changed the condition of the soil and affected microbes, a transplant fertilizer or root stimulant such as kelp may give the plant a real boost.

Transplant fertilizers or stimulants? Why complicate things? They're external commercial inputs. Build a healthy garden soil with lots of compost so you can minimize external inputs. (Feed indoors? Absolutely. But in the garden, with well-amended soil, I err on the side of cheapness.) *He said*

She said But don't forget, Steve, that kelp has growth hormones, not just nutrients.

Funny how people freak out about growth hormones in their meat, yet not when used to grow their veg...

Outdoor Seeding and Transplanting Q+A

My soil gets so hard the seeds don't seem to be able to sprout or push their way through. Why?

She said A crusty soil makes for a crusty gardener. Clay is very often a contributing factor, but don't let it make you crusty! Many gardeners point an accusing finger at clay, but most often the problem is too little organic matter.

Real Vegetable Gardeners Don't...

Real vegetable gardeners don't fret if they miss a seeding date.

They seed anyway, to see whether the crop will still grow well—or plant something else instead.

He said

> This year I missed the boat when it came to planting my fall cabbage. But I threw down some rapini seed instead—as it will be ready in less time.

Real vegetable gardeners don't try to squeeze every last transplant into the garden.

Whether you grow or buy transplants, in most cases you'll end up with extras. That's good...because it allows you to ruthlessly pick only the best plants for the garden. What about the others, you ask? Compost them!

Summary: Outdoor Seeding and Transplanting

Everything need not be planted on one magical day in spring. Instead, seed frost-hardy plants first, covering them if necessary, and follow-up with semi-frost-hardy seedlings, and, finally, frost-tender seeds and seedlings. Enjoy the whole spring planting experience a bit at a time.

Donna and Steve's Thumbs-Up Guide

GUFF AND GARDENING STUFF		DONNA	STEVE
1. Climate	Row Covers	Up	Down
	Cold Frames	Up	Up
2. Soil	Rotating Composters	Up	Down
	Rototilling	Down	Up
3. Planning	Planning Perfectionism	Down	Down
	Flowers Mixed with Veg	Up	Up
4. Garden Making	Pythagorean Theorem	Up	Down
	Double Digging	Down	Down
5. Crop Selection	Broad Beans	Down	Up
	Asparagus Pea	Down	Down
	Rotation	Up	Down
6. Indoor Seeding	Peat-Based Soilless Mixes	Up	Up
	Fine Textured Seeding Mixes	Up	Down
	Coir-Based Mixes	Down	Down
7. Seeding + Transplanting	Sorrel	Up	Up
	Root Stimulants	Up	Down

Garden Coaches Chat: No guff. Lots of fun.
for more details visit www.GardenCoachesChat.com

8 GARDEN MAINTENANCE

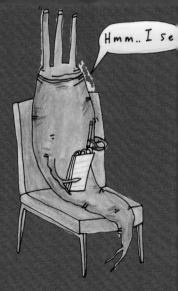

Hmm.. I se

Top 3 Sensible Maintenance Tips

1. Proper nutrition starts with a healthy soil.

2. When adding external inputs, remember soil microbes.

3. Don't sweat it! But be prepared to accept some loss to pests—and don't let that affect your enjoyment of gardening.

Some Gardener Psychology to Start

We don't pretend to be psychologists: we're plant-loving horticulturists. But we're not totally blind to human ways and have noticed that there are different types of gardeners with different motives and objectives. If you think we're talking guff right now, we're not. We point this out because motives and objectives have a big effect on how much care a gardener will likely give the garden.

Type 1

"I just want to make sure I have at least 40 hours of work to do each week," said one of Donna's clients when they met about his garden shortly after he retired.

For some people, vegetable gardens expand and grow to fill the time and space allocated. It is the process as much as actual production for these Type 1 gardeners. Some of them measure success in yields, but most fanatics simply want to garden. They would do it even if they were banned from eating all the food.

He said Admission: this sounds like me, Donna.

Type 2

"I want to make sure it is low maintenance," say most of Donna's clients, who plan to outsource the work, saying they are busy, or will be away for the summer, but want to have a small vegetable area.

The Type 2 gardener plants as a demonstration for kids or neighbours. Such gardeners are usually looking for something recognizable, such as a carrot or tomato, for garden produce rather

than the garden experience. Buying and planting a single tomato with fruit already on it is one way to be realistic about time for Type 2 gardeners.

Type 3

Type 3 gardeners are looking for the social experience and they are the ones who organize local community gardens and seed swaps. They help friends in the garden, even when their own needs attention.

A gardener's leaning towards a particular "type" might flip-flop with the time of the person's life and even with the time of day or day of the week. It might be a philosophical argument—to grow your food. Or it might be an entry point to something bigger… a single tomato in a pot growing into a fiendish desire to fill all the space with edibles.

Whether you're a type 1, 2, or 3 gardener, we want to drive home the point that you should never begrudge maintenance time. It's time that gives you a good opportunity to see crop stages and watch for pests.

She said
Many people practise yoga to quiet their mind. Weeding can have the same impact. Of course working in a vegetable garden can also boost your cancer fighting vitamin D levels and provide some good exercise!

He said
Forget the yoga—try braiding onions for contemplative time!

Garden Care Simplified
Spring Work

There is always more work in the spring than any other time of year, so it's not a good time for gardeners to go on holidays!

❁ Begin indoor seeding two to three months before outdoor transplanting, depending on the crop. Work back from your last average spring frost date.

She said
I start tomatoes no earlier than mid-March for outdoor planting in June in Calgary—but I need to start leeks in February if I want any crop at all.

❁ Remove weeds when young, before they form seeds.

❁ Empty the compost heap and spread it over the garden. Work compost or leaves left on the garden in fall lightly into top 5–10 cm (2–4 inches) of soil.

She said
Don't double dig now or ever.

He said
I like to work in my compost in the fall, not the spring.

❁ Rake and prepare the seedbeds. Know your soil and don't work it too early, or you risk compacting it.

She said
At this point, I spray compost tea on the soil and get the microbes working before seeding.

❁ Plant early frost-tolerant or "cheater" seeds.

❁ Monitor moisture levels, young weeds, and pests.

❁ Set out young, hardy transplants into cold frames, placing pots in cold frames or physically transplanting plants such as cabbage and broccoli into the soil in the cold frames.

❁ On or about the time of the average last spring frost date in your area, plant most of the garden.

❁ Start hardening off tender crops (such as tomatoes) that have been raised indoors, but do not leave them outside overnight yet.

❁ Direct-seed tender crops a week or so after the average last frost.

❁ Plant hardened tender crops after the above seeding. Prepare to cover them if the weather turns cold.

103

Late Spring and Summer Work

Daily Chores

❁ Walk in the garden looking for signs of growth, bugs, weeds, blooms, and dryness. This is a mostly contemplative activity done after work or supper. It develops into a mind-set (especially if you keep a garden diary and record what you see each time you tour the garden).

❁ Water as needed. Always use a spray nozzle if using a hose so that water falls gently on the soil surface and doesn't damage the soil structure. Early in the season it is better to water by hand—later you can use a sprinkler or irrigation.

Weekly Chores

❁ Scuffle the garden with a hoe or three-pronged cultivator to fluff the soil surface. This removes tiny weeds before they become a problem, aerates the soil surface, and reduces the moisture lost to the environment. Long-handled tools save your back and make the task quick and painless, but in raised beds it may be easier to sit on the side and use a hand tool.

THINNING

Assume some seeds won't germinate and plant a few extras: some are already dead in the packet; others will perish before they germinate; and some will die (or be eaten by bugs or bunnies) after they emerge. Then, if there are extra seedlings, these can be thinned after they come up.

❁ Thin out plants that are growing too close together. Carrot patches, for instance, benefit from regular thinning. Remaining plants grow so much bigger if the seedlings are thinned on a weekly basis. If there is too much kale or lettuce in an area, it can be transplanted to another spot.

❁ Begin looking for plants that need staking or tying.

❁ Harvest radishes and early lettuce and spinach. Pick off bits of herbs as needed for use in the kitchen.

❁ Add small weeds, thinned plants, and other materials to compost all season long on an ongoing basis.

❁ Stake or tie tomatoes.

❁ Water once crops are established. This is especially important for onions and garlic, as they need ample water to form a large bulb.

❁ WeeD every time you walk through the garden pull out bits and pieces.

He said I try to keep weeds from going to seed but am not a perfectionist when it comes to weeds. If you look you'll find them in my garden. I'm not embarrassed.

But....and this is an important but... if weeds have formed seeds, don't put them in your compost. Have a separate heap for such weeds—or put them out with municipal yard waste collection. When I moved to my current home, I used the compost that the previous owner left. BIG MISTAKE. I have never had so many weeds in a garden before. The reason? There were weeds that had formed seed added to that compost.

Monthly Chores

❁ Apply specialized fertilizers as needed based on plant appearance or Brix tests (see page 116).

❁ Apply compost tea monthly during the growing season.

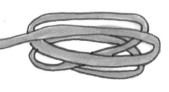

From left (pg. 104-105): baby greens are harvested before plants mature; tomatoes staked with iron rebar; thin beets shortly after they sprout; grow cucumbers on a trellis; bountiful cantaloupe and eggplant harvest; tomato stakes in teepee formation.

What's Sweet: The Great Tomato Debate

Many gardeners have tried-and-true tomato-growing techniques and defend them fiercely. This is one debate unlikely to ever be resolved—and we certainly won't try. Below we've noted some of the good and not-so-good aspects of four common approaches to growing tomatoes.

SYSTEM	SWEET	NOT SO SWEET
Caging	❀ No need to prune and train as with staked tomatoes ❀ Keeps tomatoes off the ground, meaning less rot and cleaner fruit ❀ In cool spring weather a cage can be encircled with clear plastic to create a mini-greenhouse	❀ The need to anchor cages to the ground with stakes to prevent toppling ❀ Hard to buy cages that are big enough for tomato plants and with holes through which hands can fit for picking
Sprawling	❀ The easiest way to grow tomatoes ❀ No supplies needed	❀ Rot and bugs find tomatoes on the ground ❀ Requires more space ❀ Tomatoes often hidden under a tangle of vines.
Staking	❀ Keeps tomatoes off the ground, meaning less rot and cleaner fruit ❀ Fits more plants into a row ❀ Pruning usually results in larger fruit ❀ Fruit easier to find and pick ❀ Stakes easy to buy and install	❀ Staking and pruning takes time—lots of it ❀ Fewer tomatoes ❀ The hassle of end-of-season take-down
Trellising	❀ Keeps tomatoes off the ground, meaning less rot and cleaner fruit ❀ A bit less pruning and tying than staking	❀ As with staking, setting up stakes and pruning takes time—and with trellising there's the need to install wires too ❀ The hassle of end-of-season take-down

BLANCHING

Like dying hair, blanching crops is more about fashion than it is about having a healthier crop. By keeping some of the plant out of the sun, it remains white—and the flavour may also be milder.

Blanching often involves burying parts of the plant. Leeks and celery are hilled with soil to increase the white part of the stalk. Celery that has not been hilled is distinctly greener than hilled celery. Asparagus is another crop that can be hilled. In other cases, plants are shaded. Placing a board over endive for five days will cause the leaves to go white. Individual dandelions may be covered with a heavy clay pot or soil.

She said I don't hill celery—I like the sharp flavour.

He said This is all a bit much for me. I'm happy with green vegetables.

She said My friend Marinette moved to Canada from France. She remembers when she was a little girl in France, her father took her to a farmer's field a week or so after it had been ploughed to look for dandelions that had been turned under. These plants were not dead, just inadvertently blanched from being buried. Dandelions are bitter if green, but once blanched the leaves are pale yellow and delicious in salads.

Compost Tea

The idea behind compost tea is to multiply the good microbes found in compost. These microbes are grown in a "tea" solution that is applied to the soil to build up the good microbes already on site or to add or repopulate soil if it is microbe-poor.

Bucket Brewed Tea

Some people make compost tea by putting fresh manure in a bucket (also known as the poop-in-a-bucket method). Some prescribe occasional stirring. These bucket systems do not provide much aeration of the tea, which could cause a...microbial mess. Instead of beneficial microbes, harmful ones—ones that grow in the absence of air—might proliferate.

She said One gardener told me about using bucket-method compost tea that killed his tomato crop. Of course, that's an extreme case, but it's the reason I do not advise these systems.

Aearated Tea

To make compost tea with a good microbial balance, some gardeners use commercial aerobic brewers that move air bubbles through the brewing tea. Serious compost-tea gardeners might add carbohydrates or minerals to feed and grow the populations of beneficial microbes. High-quality compost tea takes about 24 hours to make and it should be used promptly, while good microbes dominate.

Not-Really Tea

Products seeping out of a manure or compost pile are not compost tea—they are compost leachates. Without a laboratory test, you can't tell what they contain. Don't bother using them for tea.

He said Let me guess: there's probably an expensive gadget for making compost tea, right?

She said Definitely! I am on my second tea maker now, and I am looking under the microscope with each batch to make sure it has plenty of good microbes.

He said I say thumbs down on the compost tea. Neat idea, but I don't have time for it. (And if I did, I might use a fish tank bubbler in a bucket...)

MAKE A CLEAN STAKE

There are many things that work as stakes, from branches to old hockey sticks to recycled goods. What irks both of us is the tropical hardwood stakes so often seen at garden retailers. Hello…we live in a country with lots of wood, so why bring in stakes from a distant rainforest?

He said I've tried wooden strapping, which is cheap…but like any wooden stake, it rots with time. I've had best long-term results with iron rebar. I think plastic-coated metal stakes are overpriced.

She said I buy the plastic-coated metal stakes because they do not rot, rust, or snap-and they're ridged.

Thumbs-Down Garden Tools Guide
We each have tools we don't use. Here's why.

TOOL	COACH	THUMBS	WHY?
Leaf blower	Donna and Steve	Down	Because they're too loud, too loud, too loud, and they emit exhaust. We prefer the rake.
Hoe (all types)	Steve	Down	Because I plant mainly in dense blocks. While many gardeners use a hoe to scuffle the soil between rows of plants, I don't have rows. And I cover walkways with straw to suppress weeds.
Hoe (potato)	Donna	Down	Because the potato hoe is strictly for hilling potatoes. I prefer the more versatile circle hoe, triangle hoe, and loop hoe for various light weeding and soil fluffing around the yard.
Hand-held seeder	Steve	Down	Because I plant in blocks and don't need perfectly spaced rows.

Plant Nutrition: What is it?

Plant nutrition starts with the sun. That's because plants grab energy from sunlight. Then, using that energy, they collect the other building blocks required to grow.

Good human nutrition means balancing energy-supplying carbohydrates with bodybuilding protein, system-scrubbing fibre, and vitamins and minerals—all from different sources. For plants, good nutrition is a bit simpler: it's squarely based on mineral elements in the soil. That's because plants manufacture protein and vitamins and carbohydrates.

Sorry if mineral elements sounds like technical jargon, but the word elements does a pretty good job of describing what plants take from the soil. By elements, we mean stuff like nitrogen, phosphorus, and potassium: these are the

macro-elements, meaning plants require a considerable amount of them. Then there are trace elements such as calcium, iron, and zinc—which plants need, but in smaller quantities.

Elements can exist in different forms. If you're a chemist, you'll be excited by all these forms. If you're a gardener…don't feel you have to be. Beyond being a strictly chemical equation, plant nutrition involves biological processes too. There are all sorts of microbes and biological processes that affect the cycling and availability of these elements to plants.

So what practical conclusion can you, the gardener, draw from what we've said above? Here are the main things that we want to point out:

VITAMINS

❋ Veggies need sun to get their energy for growth.

❋ Most elements needed for good plant growth are in a well-maintained soil.

❋ By building a healthy soil with lots of organic matter and biological activity, you help make sure the elements in the soil are available to plants.

❋ Constantly making withdrawals (i.e. harvests) from the soil bank may lead to a negative balance. Again, compost is the solution. Make it and use it liberally.

107

Microbes and Soil Nutrition: Backgrounder

Partying Bacteria and Nitrogen

If the heading nutrition makes you think of eating, you're on the right track. There's lots of eating and consuming going on in vegetable garden soil.

Let's start with the role of soil bacteria in the world of plant nutrition. Like us (and you too), bacteria have nitrogen in their bodies. Think of soil bacteria in two ways:

- **Bacterial Introverts**: Known as rhizobium bacteria, these are the oh-so-reserved bacteria that don't like to mingle, so they stay around home, which happens to be a plant root with which they're having an amorous fling.

- **Bacterial Extroverts:** These are the free-living, free-wheeling free agents in the bacterial world. They party their way around soil or compost.

These bacterial introverts and extroverts play a pivotal role in the availability of nitrogen—a major plant nutrient—to our vegetable crops.

- Nitrogen-catching rhizobium bacteria present in soil associate with peas and beans (and other legumes).

- Free-living bacteria are ingested by protozoa, which in turn excrete nitrogen as a waste product into the soil.

Like birds nibbling on berries, protozoa eat bacteria in the soil. Lots of bacteria make lots of food for protozoa, make lots of eating and excreting…you get the picture. With a healthy, microbe-energized soil, there is often enough nitrogen available for plants without the addition of outside inputs from either commercial or organic fertilizers.

I had so many protozoa in my worm castings that the available nitrogen was off the map! My castings sample **She said** *had over one million protozoa when the average expected by the testing lab per sample was just over 10,000.*

Other Microbes and Elements at the Party

Sometimes at a party it takes that special person to get the atmosphere right—to get people interacting and sharing stories. In the soil, there are many fungi (plural of fungus) that do the same thing. What they do is alter the acidity of the soil in the area immediately around plant roots (known as the rhizosphere). By doing that, they set the mood: they get the party happening and help plant roots mingle with the nutrients they seek.

The matchmaking isn't limited to acidity in the rhizosphere. Some fungi work as translators, making otherwise unavailable calcium available to plants. This translating—this diplomacy—is important because calcium is used by plants in cell walls, where it provides strength. And strong cell walls are physically harder for insects such as aphids to pierce.

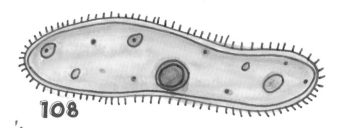

108

IT'S A COMPLICATED PARTY...DON'T SWEAT IT

Professional growers who believe in harnessing the microbial power of the soil for feeding plants might use soil advisors to help make decisions about rotation, cover crops, and inputs to optimize nutrition. Home gardeners have to sort it all out by themselves.

Rotating crops, using cover crops, and encouraging microbes all helps to balance plant nutrition—but some elements can still become deficient. After all, as we harvest, we remove elements that were once in the soil. The point is that there can be so many interrelated factors, there's not always one simple answer about how one factor can affect one nutrient.

SPOTTING NUTRITION PROBLEMS

Ever noticed how older leaves turn yellow at the bottom of the plant sometimes? That can be a sign that the plant is short on nitrogen. The plant moves the mobile nitrogen when it's needed in new growth. It's supply and demand in the plant world. Put out a call for nitrogen and it is moved where it is needed.

Luckily, not all nutrient deficiencies look the same. With some elements, new leaves are discoloured; with some, the discoloration is just between the veins. (This is the case with iron deficiencies.) With some, it may be a colour other than yellow: phosphorus deficiency combined with cool weather can turn leaves purple. This happens in the early spring when otherwise hardy plants are struggling to root into cool soil right after they are transplanted.

What we're getting at is that in some cases, it is possible to make a good guess about what's ailing our plants, just by the type of discoloration we see in the leaves.

Feeding Plants and Soil

Compost and Castings as Food

She said I make a lot of compost. I also use worm castings to make compost tea and apply it in the spring to the soil, and again when the plants are growing, for a total of two or three times per season. In some ways this is a homeopathic system—surely there isn't much actual value or quantity of food in an aerated but highly diluted compost tea? It is hard to know for sure: the references don't even agree, but I believe this will lead to better soil. In my mind, everything comes back to the same thing: building soil.

He said I don't feed regularly throughout the summer with composts or teas. To me, it seems like a lot of work. Instead, I work compost into the soil in the fall, as I prepare the garden for the following spring.

From top: magnesium deficiency appears as pale raised spots between veins; blossom-end rot on tomatoes linked to calcium availability.

Commercial Fertilizers

He said I remember when I worked at a horticultural supply company. We sold all sorts of stuff including biological controls, pots...and fertilizer. One summer, with a garden full of fine-looking tomatoes, I took a few to work to share. The biggest of those tomatoes really did look like a little pumpkin. Little did I know that on that same day some of the top brass would be there, and would ask which of the inorganic fertilizers had given me such results. I gulped and said that I used shrimp compost—not the fertilizers we sold.

That's not to say I'm opposed to inorganic fertilizers in principle, but I am opposed to their overuse—or use to the exclusion of soil-building organic matter. While a compost-driven garden with great soil probably doesn't need them—in container culture, where the nutrient pool is limited, they can have a place.

She said Shrimp compost has high levels of calcium-and tomatoes are sensitive to soils low in calcium, so Steve did his tomato crop a huge favour adding the shrimp compost! He was also feeding soil fungi... a whole other story.

Steve's son Quinn loves worms.

He said OK, you might have noticed I'm not on board with the products to the right. It's not that I'm against them all in principle, but I don't see the need in my home garden. I'm not commercially raising veggies, and I just don't see the point. There are so many neat products available, but they come at a price. Leaf and kitchen compost cost me nothing but my time and labour. If I lived next to the ocean, maybe I'd use seaweed and kelp.

THINKING ABOUT SYNTHETIC, INORGANIC, ORGANIC, AND NATURAL FERTILIZERS

He said I often hear people talking about organic fertilizer as if it's innocuous and synthetic fertilizer as if it's the devil. Instead of getting hung up on organic fundamentalism, try using fewer external inputs. And ask questions about those you do buy—organic or not.

To me, no-guff gardening is less about external inputs such as fertilizers, and more about the soil—a systems approach that has a healthy soil as its foundation. I've seen some so-called organic fertilizers that are so dilute and bulky that I hate to think how much packaging—and how much fuel for transportation—has been used. Wouldn't it be better to simply use compost from your own garden?

She said I occasionally use organic fertilizers. But the point is this: if you are going to grow organically, you need to adopt a whole new way of gardening. Simply switching to organic fertilizers does not an organic gardener make. I agree with Steve that you have to first fix the soil and that might easily be done with compost alone.

She said I use products such as kelp, humic acids, and fish fertilizers because I believe these products do no harm to garden plants or soils while they supply trace elements and carbohydrates to feed microbes, which, in turn, feed the I guess it's true-I'll try anything once.

COACHES' THUMBS-UP GUIDE TO NUTRITIONAL PRODUCTS

SUPPLEMENT	THUMBS	WHAT IS IT	HOW APPLIED	WHAT IT DOES	NOTES
Alfalfa Pellets	Up / Down	High quality alfalfa hay compressed into pellets. Usually sold as bunny or pet food. A full meal deal!	Top-dress or broadcast on soil or planting beds in spring just before or after seeding.	Like adding green manure, alfalfa supplies small amounts of major and trace elements to soil.	Easy to use, alternative to other fertilizers. It also provides organic matter to soil. Will "heat" compost pile if used in place of manures or green grass.
Black Strap Molasses	Up / Down	Sugar.	Mixed with water it can be added to compost or compost tea.	Feeds microbes, providing energy and allowing them to multiply.	Do not add directly to soil. May feed bad (or anaerobic) microbes, so make sure compost-tea maker is oxygenated.
Fish Fertilizer	Up / Down	Waste fish parts ground up and stabilized with phosphoric acid.	Watered into soil or sprayed on plants.	Provides a broad spectrum of elements in a single application.	There is a smell, and fishy taste may transfer to food such as strawberries if applied just before harvest. May be used in compost or compost tea instead of directly in garden.
Gypsum	Skeptical / Down	A dry product that adds calcium and sulphur to soil without making it sweeter or raising pH.	Top-dress or broadcast, and then cultivate into soil.	Some people believe it "softens" soil by replacing lost calcium.	
Humic and Fulvic Acids	Up / Down	Usually a mined product, a poor quality coal of some description.	Sold as both a dry powder and liquid concentrate. Can be applied to compost piles to feed microorganisms or watered into garden.	Provides carbon. Reported to favour growth of fungus in a compost pile. Might boost root production.	Although there are products sold as humic and fulvic acids, the most prolific humate producers are fungus. Dry leaves + fungus = lots of humic acid.
Lime	Down / Down	Calcium or magnesium carbonate.	Top-dress or broadcast, then cultivate into the soil.	"Sweetens" soil, making it more alkaline. Also prescribed for acidic soils low in available calcium or magnesium.	Don't use this without further information. Many soils already have a high pH. Never use non-agricultural limes. If the soil is already sweet, adding lime is like adding extra soap to soapy water.
Rock Dust, Rock Phosphate, Carbonitite	Skeptical / Down	Various sources so product can vary. Most often cited as food for microbes.	Add to compost or to soil and work in. May be added to compost tea.	Provides phosphorus and other trace elements to microbes, which in turn die and make it available to plant roots.	This is a highly complex and possibly misleading area. Donna is trialling various materials and has read a ton, but is still skeptical. The good news is it probably won't cause trouble and might be good.
Seaweed and Kelp	Up / Down	Seaweed and aquatic plants.	Sprayed on in liquid form, spread in dry form as meal or actual kelp spread on soil or added to compost.	Very dilute fertilizer containing major and trace elements. Stimulates more root mass. Natural plant hormones occur in seaweed, helping break dormancy in seeds and encouraging germination.	Can be an activator in compost because it stimulates bacterial growth. Often sold in combination with humic and fulvic acids.

WEEDS

What Is A Weed?

A weed is nothing more than a plant growing where it's unwanted. Dill can become a weed if allowed to reseed everywhere—while dandelions are a favourite edible plant for many. Weeds can have a considerable effect on yield by competing with your crops for light, water, and space.

You can classify weeds in two broad groups: **annual** and **perennial**. The reason you might want to know whether a weed is annual or perennial is that it can affect your control strategy.

JERUSALEM ARTICHOKE:

The Vegetable That's a Weed

Jerusalem artichokes, also called sunchokes, are a tasty root vegetable. But the plant is also very bossy—so much so, that it's classed as a weed in some jurisdictions.

She said My worst weed is actually a tree. My inner city garden is surrounded by trees. While weeding out little Manitoba maple seedlings one spring with my four-year-old granddaughter, I explained that these little seedlings were actually weeds and they came from the neighbour's tree. Mali, looking up at the offending tree, said, "We should go tell the neighbour his weeds are in our garden."

He said My worst weed is ground ivy, also known as gill-over-the-ground. It's a perennial with creeping stems that root at every node. It spreads rapidly and fills unfilled— and planted—areas with ease.

Right: Donna's grandson Kale loves dandelion seed heads.

Weed Control Strategies

Cultivation

For annual weeds, cultivating can work quite well. Tilling or scuffling the soil is often enough to set back annual weeds or kill them. If you have chickweed, make sure to turn the soil as soon as weeds germinate. Larger plants can break into parts and regrow or reseed.

She said I love my winged weeder for scuffling out weeds. OK, my loop hoe is a favourite too. And the circle hoe.

For perennial weeds such as thistle, horsetail, and dandelion, careless cultivation can worsen the problem. That's because digging can break up the roots into small pieces, and each has the potential to grow into a new plant. With such perennial weeds, careful digging to remove as much of the root system as possible is necessary. Be persistent.

Pulling

Some annual weeds can be yanked out by hand. After a rain, when the soil is moist, you can pull out many annual weeds and get most of the root system.

He said I tend to do a lot of pulling as I plant dense blocks where I can't easily cultivate with a hoe or tiller.

Left: dandelions are deep rooted perennials.

Physical Barriers

Some people grow crops such as tomatoes and melons with a layer of plastic on top of the soil to catch heat and to smother weed growth. After the plastic is in place, a slit is made, through which the plant is placed in the soil. Anyone who has seen a quack grass root grow through asphalt knows plastic is not a permanent solution to this perennial weed but it is worth a try.

Likewise, a thick layer of mulch or compost can cover weed seeds or seedlings and may be enough to slow or stop their growth or at least stop the germination of weeds that need light to germinate.

She said

Be careful, though, as some mulches (e.g. evergreen bark chips) tie up soil nutrients and may give off toxins to plants. I use bark chips between the rows of raised beds but not on the garden soil itself.

He said

I've had good success snuffing out perennial thistles using landscape fabric.

Dense Planting

With a thick stand of tomatoes or peas or beans, there aren't many weeds that grow vigorously. The reason is simple: there isn't enough light and moisture for strong weed growth. This strategy is all about out-competing the weeds. Another way to out-compete weeds is to use green-manure crops on empty patches.

Herbicides

Herbicides: a lot of gardeners cringe at the mention of a word ending in "cide," so we probably have your attention. No guff, herbicide is not a dirty word. It just means an agent that kills plants:

- A kettle full of boiling water has good herbicidal properties and can scald away hard-to-pull weeds in areas such as flagstone pathways.

- Vinegar is an acid with herbicidal properties, and will burn leaves of many plants.

- Corn gluten meal can be used as a herbicide because it contains compounds that affect root growth in germinating seeds.

While boiling water and vinegar kill top growth, neither kills the roots of weeds. Weeds with strong roots—especially perennial weeds—will regrow.

Edible Weeds:
Can't Beat Em, Eat Em

Eating weeds is far from a control strategy, but makes you look at them in a different way. If you eat them, are they still weeds? Good question!

He said

In the spring I like to find young dandelion greens to mix in with salad greens. Purslane, too, is edible...though I can't say I'm crazy about it.

She said

Have I mentioned I like my dandelions crisp-as in deep-fried?

Weeds as a Diagnostic Tool

Some gardeners look to weed populations as an indication of soil health. For example, soils with dandelions might be low in calcium-attracting fungus or too high in potassium (which has displaced calcium on the clay sites). Calcium is mobile once it is displaced on the clay particle, and can leach out of reach of shallow vegetable roots.

He said

I think the concept of weeds as a diagnostic tool is very exciting but am skeptical about its practical application in the home vegetable garden.

VINEGAR AS A HERBICIDE

Household vinegar is a 5 per cent formulation of acetic acid—not as strong as commercial acetic-acid weed-control products. Acetic acid herbicides may slow down weeds by killing leaves, but they do not kill the roots of the weed, so plants with strong roots will likely regrow—making repeat treatments necessary.

ack

Bugs and Critters

As Steve pulled off the blue Tupperware lid with one hand, he shook the salad dressing in the other. Then, without looking, he doused his homegrown garden salad. Readying his fork, he was surprised to see that he had dressed more than the salad: like a marching army, oil-and-vinegar-dressed aphids were parading around.

Being hungry, at work, and far from any cafeteria, he ate his salad, flicking off aphids with his fork as he ate (much to the amusement of colleagues). It was one of his first experiences with edible flowers. It was also a good lesson on the importance of washing food, as aphids love nasturtiums and had concealed themselves in the nasturtium flowers in the salad.

Common Insect Pests In The Vegetable Garden

There are many ways to slice a tomato...and many ways to deal with pests. Healthy plants are a good starting point for fewer pests—though there are always flare-ups that can happen. Instead of prescribing theory, here we'll tell you how each of us handles pest problems.

Having read our respective approaches to insects, you'll notice that we're not control freaks—and that we don't aspire to picture-perfect produce from our gardens. Having said that, we hold that in a well-managed vegetable garden, you will get great-looking produce without swarms of bugs.

Clockwise: (1) nasturtium blooms attract aphids; (2) slug; (3) slug-damaged leaf; (4) rabbit-hewn chard; (5) tomato transplant with protective paper collar; (6) cabbage moth larvae; (7) weevils on dry beans; (8) cabbage ravaged by cabbage moth larvae; (9) squirrel-munched tomato.

PEST	STEVE SAYS	DONNA SAYS
Aphids:	Aphid colonies quickly attract predators, so I look for these—and, if there are enough predators that I think the aphid numbers will be mowed down quick enough, I leave well enough alone. Otherwise, I spot spray with insecticidal soap.	Aphids focus on new growth where nitrogen levels are high, so trim off tops of affected plants. Stop adding so much nitrogen fertilizer.
Cabbage Root Maggot	I've never had them (that I know of)!	Plants in the cabbage family suddenly wilt shortly after being planted out in spring—even if they have plenty of water. My son-in-law, when told the cause of the wilt in his cauliflower patch, promptly pulled up all of the affected plants, washed the roots, and replanted. With success.
Cabbage Worms:	I grow broccoli with small florets (enough florets to sacrifice a couple to bugs). And I grow a fall crop, because the worms don't do much damage then.	I use row covers. I have also been trialling high-Brix fertilizers. (See page 116 for more about Brix.)
Carrot Rust Flies:	I don't do anything against carrot rust flies, so I get the odd carrot with holes—and I just cut out the holes.	I don't (but could) use row covers.
Cucumber Beetles:	I live with them.	I haven't had them.
Cutworms:	I use newspaper collars around the tomato transplants I've slaved over. I don't protect other plants from cutworms and accept occasional losses.	I have suggested toilet paper rolls as collars but have not used them myself. This is a pest easily controlled with the biological insecticide Bt if it is applied when small. Toilet paper rolls? I thought you were to embarrassed to use them to grow seedlings indoors!
Earwigs:	They're without a doubt the ugliest bug in my garden. They love to hide out in heads of lettuce. I soak the lettuce before putting it in the fridge—and that usually encourages them to come out of hiding.	Have not had a problem—so far—but then again I garden in a cool climate.
Flea Beetles:	I grow arugula before or after flea beetle season. I don't worry about them on crops such as radish.	Row covers help but I don't want to cover everything, so I don't worry about the tiny holes they leave in radish, bok choy, and other greens.
Leaf Miners:	I don't worry about leaf miner damage to chard, and just cut it out.	I just remove damaged pieces of leaf before cooking.
Onion Maggots:	Never knowingly had them.	Pupae overwinter in soil so move onions to new spot each spring. Also, remove onions from garden in fall so there is no food source first thing in spring.
Potato Beetles:	I pick them off by hand on the rare occasion that they visit.	Not a problem.
Slugs:	Same approach as earwigs: soak lettuce heads in a pail of water before bringing into the kitchen to get out the slugs.	Water less often. Put down boards and scrape slugs off in the morning.
Spider Mites:	I rarely get these in the veggie garden.	Only a problem on greenhouse plants for me. Wash plants and use beneficial insects early.
Tomato Hornworm:	I have never once had a tomato hornworm.	Not a problem but easily hand picked.
Wireworms:	Not a problem.	A problem with root crops in new gardens only. Wireworms were there in the soil when there was a lawn, but once the lawn is gone and the juicy carrot or beet roots are the only offerings, wireworms jump in and feast. No solution but time.

SECURITY BARRIERS FOR BUGS

We'll pass on the tear gas, but take a cue from police forces when it comes to other means of crowd control: security barriers for cabbage root maggots and carrot rust flies.

The method is called an exclusion fence. The basis of this technique is simple: Few adults of these pest species fly more than a metre off the ground, so many of them can be foiled by a simple fence. OK, it's not just any fence: It's a one-metre-high fence of nylon window screen placed around the garden bed, with the bottom edge buried in the soil. The top 30 cm (12 inches) of the fence is folded outwards (away from the bed) because such an overhang deflects the more ambitious of these faint-hearted flyers.

Linda Gilkeson, author of the book, Backyard Bounty: The Complete Guide to Year-Around Organic Gardening in the Pacific Northwest, says she has tried exclusion fences and row covers. "Having tried both methods, I have to say the floating row covers are much, much easier to put in place, though there is a 'laundry-on-the-garden' look to them that isn't great. Both methods work only if you rotate crops to make sure there are no root maggots still in the soil from a previous crop."[1]

1   Backyard Bounty: The Complete Guide to Year-Around Organic Gardening in the Pacific Northwest. 2011. Linda Gilkeson. New Society Publishers.

Insect Control Strategies

Don't Encourage Them

It may sound obvious, but when we say don't encourage them, we mean growing fewer crops that are prone to insect damage, or growing crops in situations that don't invite damage. Flea beetles, which gnaw small holes in crops such as arugula, can be foiled by growing the crop before beetles emerge—or after the beetles are mostly gone for the season.

Exclude Insects

Sometimes it's possible to exclude insect pests using a physical barrier. A newspaper collar around young transplants prevents cutworms from reaching them. Cabbage root maggots can be excluded using a 20 cm (8 inch) square piece of tarpaper or cardboard at the base of the plant, preventing the adult from laying eggs next to the plant, where it wants to. Row covers keep crops warm, but they also keep out some bugs.

He said Did I hear you say tar paper in the garden, Donna?

Keep Plant Brix Levels High

Brix is a measure of dissolved sugars, and Brix measurements were used first by grape growers but are gradually being adopted by farmers and gardeners. Brix levels tell grape farmers when fruit is ripe. A high Brix measurement is a good indication of flavour, and in good conditions, grapes will have better or higher readings. Many consider Brix a sign of something more than just flavour: they consider it an indication of plant health. And a healthy plant is less susceptible to insect damage.

She said I have started experimenting with high-Brix fertilizers and an instrument called a refractometer to measure plant Brix levels. If increases in plant sugars are linked to pest resistance, so much the better. I don't fully understand why plants are not as attractive to insects when they have higher Brix readings, but so far my results have been positive. In my initial year of trialling the product, I had Brussels sprouts that were buggy early in the season, but when we harvested them in late fall, they were clean. No pests. No signs of pests on the sprouts. On a cabbage family plant that is a miracle.

He said The logic makes sense...but I'm not buying a refractometer for a home vegetable garden.

Alyssum flowers feed beneficial insects.

Extermination

We're not extermination fanatics. You've probably gathered that by now. But sometimes it's necessary to control a bug infestation. Exterminating bugs can be done mechanically—by hand picking, for example—or can be accomplished by applying a product, an insecticide.

Mechanical Extermination

This method is easiest with larger insects such as tomato hornworm or asparagus and potato beetles. Pick off and squish adults, and smear any eggs you find on the plants.

> **He said**
> My favourite memory of low-cost extermination involves my neighbour Dimitrios, who was troubled by earwigs and would catch them every night by leaving out bundles of twigs, in which they would congregate. Then, every morning, he'd shake out the bundles and do an earwig jig on the driveway as he attempted to squish them before they scurried away.

Insecticides

Insecticides are substances that kill insects. There are natural or synthetic ones and broad-spectrum and highly targeted ones. Soap is an example of a broad-spectrum insecticide that kills most insects.

From top: ladybugs mating; yellow ladybug eggs and white, stalked lacewing eggs; ladybug larvae are black.

Nicotine, pyrethrum, and rotenone are among the more common botanical insecticides. Sometimes called "natural insecticides," because they are extracted from plants or plant parts, many people think they have no effects on humans or non-target insects.

> **He said**
> It's smoking taken to the next level: when I sold greenhouse supplies, we sold a nicotine bomb that would kill everything in the greenhouse—applicators included if they didn't get out in time.

Microbial pesticides employ bacteria or fungi to kill offending pests. Bt is the name used for a bacteria-containing insecticide that kills caterpillars of moths and butterflies such as cabbage loopers. Some microbial pesticides can be tricky to keep alive… and are sold out of refrigerators!

> **She said**
> I'm only in favour of hand picking insects. Botanical and natural products are still killers of beneficial insects. I have used diatomaceous earth in select cases, but a word of caution for the applicator: it can be dangerous if inhaled.

> **He said**
> I used to sell pesticides, so I'm no stranger to them. But I don't advise using more than insecticidal soap in the home veggie garden. Why? Because I think that a home garden should be low input. I'm not convinced you'll save a bundle of money growing vegetables—but you definitely shouldn't spend a bundle on pest-control products, organic or not.

117

STEVE USES SOAP FOR APHIDS

Here's Steve's approach to using insecticidal soap on broad beans—and if you've grown broad beans, you know that there's a good chance you may get an aphid infestation.

* Decide whether the bug infestation has arrived late enough that it won't significantly affect yield—in which case there's little point spraying. If most of the beans are formed and fairly plump, spraying is nothing but a vindictive measure.

* If it's worth spraying, have a look for beneficial insects. In the case of aphids, for example, look for parasitized aphids and aphid predators before spraying. See page 119 more about predators and parasites.

The trick with soaps is contact—thoroughly contacting the insects. Thorough coverage is important—and repeat application is needed if the pests reappear, as soap does not usually kill insect eggs.

If the predators are at work, it may not be worth spraying. But I'm not going to wait around hoping that predators will arrive before my crop is ruined. It doesn't work that way.

Mind the bees-which means spraying in the evening. I don't have a place for insecticidal soap in my garden. It is a broad-spectrum insecticide so will kill both good and bad bugs.

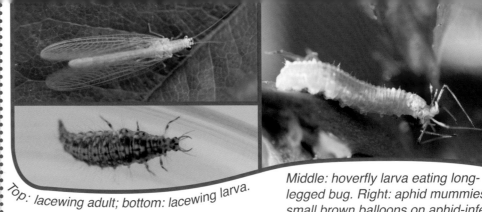

Top: lacewing adult; bottom: lacewing larva.

Middle: hoverfly larva eating long-legged bug. Right: aphid mummies look like small brown balloons on aphid-infested cabbage.

Bug-Foiling Bugs

These are the bugs we want to visit our garden. They make a buffet (or breeding ground) out of pockets of pesky insects.

Bugs are big business in agriculture. Commercial growers—especially in vegetable greenhouses—often use them as a key element of pest-control programs. Some of these bugs are predators, some are parasites—and sometimes they're referred to as beneficial insects or biocontrols. Buying commercially reared bugs for the home vegetable garden is neither low-input nor low cost.

Luckily, there are a host of different predatory and parasitic bugs that arrive on their own steam to help with your pest problems. By learning what they look like, you can protect them once you spot them. If you know they're about, mind what you apply to the plants—even soap or oil can kill them.

A Dose of Realism

Will beneficial insects control all of your pest problems? No. There's often a lead-time required for the population of beneficial insect to become large enough to control the pests… and in some cases that lead-time may require leaving your crop under siege for too long.

Parasites typically take longer to clean up an infestation than predators because they dispatch one bug per parasite egg—while predators will each gobble up countless bugs.

TOTALLY STRESSED OUT? BUGS KNOW

We walked the fields with David Cohlmeyer, market gardener and owner of Cookstown Greens. While David farms organically, he uses "natural" insecticides sparingly. His explanation? Once the soil is tip-top, insect problems diminish. He considers insect pests one of the easier problems to deal with on his farm.

It's a neat approach: reduce stresses to the plant, which in turn keeps bugs at bay. There's science behind this approach: Research indicates that aphids among plants stressed by lack of water grow and reproduce at a faster rate. It's not only a lack of food or water that can stress out plants: Overly fertile soil induces a growing frenzy in the plant. Pests such as aphids, mealy bugs, and scale, thrive on plants with overly succulent growth, which is often due to high soil nitrogen levels.

SAMPLER OF BUG-STALKING BIOCONTROLS

There are oodles more, but these are a few of the more common ones that you might see.

STALKER	MISSION	INCIDENTALLY
Aphid Parasite Aphidius family	Parasitize aphids.	The female aphidius wasp lays eggs into an unsuspecting aphid. The wasp egg grows within the aphid, eventually killing it, leaving behind a brown aphid mummy. These brown mummy shells are easy to see with a hand-held magnifying glass.
Aphid predator Aphidoletes family	Gobble up aphids.	The grownups are midges and look a bit like mosquitoes, but it's the larvae that do the killing. Mama midge lays her egg all around an aphid outbreak. What hatches are orange, wormlike larvae that gobble up oodles of aphids.
Assassin Bugs	Drink bug juice from other insects.	Not nearly as discrete as parasitic wasps such as aphidius, the assassin bug is the vampire of the insect world. It simply pierces other bugs with its sharp beak. Then it sucks up their juices.
Whitefly Parasite Encarsia family	Parasitize white fly eggs.	This is a biggie in greenhouse biocontrol, but you'll often see it in the garden too. A mini wasp, the female Encarsia lays her egg right into a whitefly egg, which becomes black as it dies and the new Encarsia grows inside.
Lacewings Chrysoperla family	Snack on soft-bodied insects including aphids, thrips, small caterpillars, scale, mites, and various insect eggs.	The adults are gossamer beauties, but it's the alligator-like larvae that do the dirty work: with a curved jaw, they grab and gobble aphids…so that they've earned the nickname aphid lion.
Ladybugs	Munch soft-bodied insects such as aphids.	It's the young ones, the agile larvae, who zip around plants at a stupendous pace (for a bug, that is) and chase down soft-bodied bugs. If you're interested in studying bugs, here's a great one to start with. There are species with lots of spots, some with red spots, some with yellow. There's even a parasitic wasp that stalks ladybugs!
Nematodes	Stab and poison soil-dwelling larvae.	Nematodes are microscopic-sized worm-like critters that infest and kill soil-dwelling worm-like larvae of a few pest species. Once inside the larvae, bacteria carried by the nematode kill larvae. Visit www.GardenCoachesChat.com for more information about nematodes.
Syrphid Flies	Dine on aphids.	The adults wear a disguise to make them look a bit like wasps or bees, but they don't sting. The larvae are the bug-eaters.

He said I used to do quality control checks on biocontrols, and it wasn't bad because a batch would arrive and I'd spend an hour or so at the microscope and then be done. But when I worked in a lab, with a microscope, transferring predatory mites from leaf to leaf on a one-haired paintbrush for days on end, I started to see bugs in my sleep.

SAY IT WITH FLOWERS: ATTRACT BENEFICIAL INSECTS

Keeping beneficial insects happy helps manage problem insects in the garden. How do we keep the good guys happy? Supply a steady stream of herb, annual, perennial, tree, and weed pollen and nectar throughout the growing season. This gives insects energy, even when there are no pest insects on which to feed. That way, they're fed and watered and on standby if pest populations start to build.

Weeds such as dandelions and trees such as pussy willows supply the earliest pollen and nectar. By late spring, early blooming perennials such as hepatica, prairie crocus, and evergreen candytuft are in bloom. By summer, annual flowers such as sweet alyssum, cosmos, and calendula bloom. Herbs such as oregano, dill, rosemary, and fennel provide insect food July through late fall.

Animal Pests

Gardeners work with nature—but that doesn't mean that all gardeners love what nature brings them. In areas where wildlife is protected, the vegetable gardener has but two strategies for animals that eat vegetables: exclude animal pests from your garden—or accept them.

Sometimes it's a lot of work playing cat and mouse with animals, and acceptance is a healthier approach than frustration. That could mean not growing something such as corn, because there's not much chance of getting it before raccoons. And it might mean planting extra tomato plants, yielding enough to share with squirrels.

Common Animal Pests

Raccoons

Raccoons are smart, so forget trying to outsmart them. Fences won't keep them out, as they are nimble climbers. Some people use electric fences to exclude raccoons... but if you plan to try electric fences, check local bylaws to be sure they are permitted.

Raccoons love corn and melons. Pick melons when they're slightly under-ripe, before the fragrance tempts the raccoons. Allow them to ripen safely in the house.

> **He said**
> For a whole summer my then-toddler Emma prefaced the word raccoon with naughty—after they came in one night and polished off the yellow watermelons she was growing.

Rabbits

Kids think they're cute, but avid gardeners don't. Rabbits love peas, broccoli, and a host of other vegetable crops. You can build a knee-high chicken-wire fence around the garden. Just be warned that rabbits are good at finding any breaches, especially the young, small rabbit kittens, which can squeeze through small holes.

> **He said**
> My neighbours have probably had a giggle or two watching me chase a rabbit in circles around my garden. Beware: rabbits WILL find any small holes or gaps in a fence.

Squirrels

Aside from being amusing, they can be infuriating. Steve's friends Fariba and Shahriar garden on the 22nd floor of a condominium, yet their garden still suffers the ravages of a highly mischievous—and fearless—squirrel. Repellents don't seem to work. We have no recommendations for you, other than to grow enough to share with the squirrels.

There's no better way to rile up a room of gentle gardeners than to mention squirrels. At a recent talk Steve gave, squirrels came up in the question-and-answer session afterwards. He left feeling hopeful that a fox would take up residence nearby after one attendee told him how a neighbourhood fox had eaten at least 20 squirrels—and those remaining were too frightened to come out of the trees.

> **She said**
> I was once scolded for calling introduced squirrels "rats with tails" on CBC radio. I have used and suggested hot chilli peppers because these were suggested by the Audubon Society.

From left: deer fence; deer foiled by a fence; bunny- and bird-deterring fences; cabbage-moth-foiling covers in the field; homemade bird and bunny covers.

but some sensitive gardeners point out this might harm squirrels.

I have no hesitation calling them rats with tails...or worse. I often commiserate with neighbours Joe and Gina about the scorched-earth tactics of our neighbourhood squirrels. At least we can laugh about them: I once found them a lovely carving of a squirrel for their mantel.

> He said

DeeR

Deer must also be excluded with fencing. Wireless deer fence works...sometimes. You have to remember to change the batteries and top up the scented wick.

Don't pretend deer are feeble jumpers. Even the tiny deer on Vancouver Island can easily pop over any fence less than eight feet tall.

She said

The footprints were our first clue. The flattened and munched veggies our second. Our deer fence had been compromised! I have had better

success excluding deer at my summer home in the country...than in the city! Cities have regulations limiting the height of fences...and deer must have figured that out.

Smaller Varmints: Mice, Voles, Moles, Gophers, Groundhogs, and Rats

These smaller animal varmints cause headaches for many a gardener. For starters, avoid having long grass or masses of tall plants near your vegetable garden—thereby eliminating nesting areas and cover from predators. If your veg (especially root vegetables) are gnawed in the garden, a vole is often the culprit. If your stash of stored veggies is pillaged, very often a mouse is the responsible party. Tunnelling moles aren't even after your veggies...they want worms, but can make a mess in their quest for wrigglers. Gophers and groundhogs are also diggers, and when they move into the neighbourhood, you might want to consider putting on your work gloves and installing wire metal mesh to a depth of a couple of feet.

> He said

In my storage area, I find that the best protection from mice is an old-fashioned snap trap with peanut butter as the lure. I hate to share the peanut butter, but it really does work well. I've had neighbours who use live traps for mice so they can release them...and I just shake my head and mutter not to release them near my place.

One year I thought I had moles because of tunnels under my asparagus patch. It turned out that rats were the culprits.

Visit www.GardenCoachesChat.com to share your animal stories and tips.

THE UNEXPECTED PEST

Donna's friend Nicola was finding carrot tops strewn on the lawn. Was it a squirrel, a gopher, or a bunny causing all this trouble? She finally saw her puppy, Finn, digging carrots out of the garden—and dropping the tops on the lawn. Caught in the act!

Maintenance Guff Busted

Guff Says

Gardeners must only water plants early in the day or risk inviting disease.

GUFFAWERS RESPOND

The logic is sound…but let's be serious! How many working people have time to water the garden in the morning.

He said Don't feel guilty if you water in the evening. That's when I usually water.

Guff Says

Striking a natural balance in the garden takes care of pest problems.

GUFFAWERS RESPOND

A vegetable garden is not a natural state. If you want zero-input gardening, skip the vegetables.

Of course we're shifting the balance of plants and insects in our favour to grow vegetables. Why pretend otherwise? But we can do it wisely.

Guff Says

Vinegar is a totally safe herbicide.

GUFFAWERS RESPOND

Because it's a well-known ingredient in the kitchen, many people love the idea of using vinegar (and other acetic acid products) as a herbicide in the garden. They're comfortable with it—and, hey, if you can consume it, why worry. Besides, it's made from an organic acid (meaning it contains carbon in the molecule).

We'd simply like to point out that even a kitchen ingredient such as vinegar is not without detractions. Here's why: First, it's a non-selective herbicide, which means it will damage whatever plants it touches—be they weeds or your vegetable crops. Second, when applied as a fine spray we introduce a risk we don't have in the kitchen: inhalation. It is not lung-friendly when inhaled. So use vinegar, but do so wisely.

Guff Says

Watch out for sodium.

GUFFAWERS RESPOND

There was recently an article in a prominent gardening magazine warning readers of the risk of non-organic fertilizers with dangerously high sodium levels, citing an analysis of 28-3-4 as an example. First we're told to mind our own sodium intake, giving us twinges of guilt as we sprinkle salt on a steak…and now we're warned about sodium in the garden!

Salt is a big concern in gardening circles these days. And so it should be. That's because some fertilizers contain salts, which, in high enough concentration, affect plant growth—and soil microbes too.

So back to the demonizing of 28-3-4. It's actually a lawn fertilizer—and we don't advocate this stuff because we don't fertilize our lawns. But we want to point out that there's lots of bad—and inaccurate—press about synthetic fertilizers. An analysis of 28-3-4 points to a urea base—and there's no sodium in urea. The author confused sodium with salts.

Sodium-salt mix-ups aren't the only way gardeners are misled. There is little mention of the fact that natural fertilizers can have high salt levels too. Take City of Toronto compost: too salty for plant growth is what a 2009 test commissioned by the Toronto Star found! And plain-Jane manure can be salty too.

Don't get your blood pressure up... just mind the salt, for both you and the garden. The best solution in our books: be as low-input as you can—use homemade compost.

Guff Says

Buy ladybugs to solve your aphid problems.

GUFFAWERS RESPOND

Ladybugs are great at gobbling up aphids. Do we advocate buying ladybugs? Sorry, no ladybugs as mail-order brides.

Instead of introducing bugs from afar, support local populations with flowers for food and woodpiles or leaves for overwintering. Local ladybeetles are at work as soon as the weather warms. Just keep them happy and they will help take care of pests. It is a rare occasion where you are further ahead buying bugs than using the ones already on-call in your yard.

He said Ladybug! Ladybug! Fly away home... I worked at a supplier selling burlap bags of imported Californian ladybugs. A common observation from clients was that once released, the ladybugs...flew away.

She said I watched baby ladybugs (the tiny black larvae) munching aphids on my mom's shrubs in Qualicum Beach, B.C. early one June when it occurred to me I had aphids on my store-bought tomato plants back in Calgary. I clipped off a few branches holding numerous larvae, tucked them into my luggage, and flew home with them. I brought them directly to the affected tomatoes, newly planted in the greenhouse. Not another aphid was seen that summer.

Guff Says

If you delay planting a crop, it will foil pests.

GUFFAWERS RESPOND

Good concept, and it works sometimes. Steve likes to plant arugula late summer to foil flea beetles. But this technique is not guaranteed to work.

It really depends on the life cycle of the insect pest. Carrot rust flies, for example, can have more than one generation per year—so delayed planting isn't foolproof. Consider delayed planting when planning your garden—but don't expect to always foil bugs.

Guff Says

Keep the leftover beer from the wiener roast and set it outside in a dish so slugs will drown.

GUFFAWERS RESPOND

Sure the beer-guzzling slugs will be attracted. But they often slide on in, take a drink, and then slide out. Beer is definitely a lure, but only works as a trap when the slugs can't get out. Besides, why waste good beer.

Maintenance Q&A

I have heard that cream of wheat is great for ants in the vegetable garden. Just sprinkle it on and the whole colony will collapse after a few days.

She said I heard that too-from a caller on CBC radio. I also happened to hear that molasses mixed with water poured on an anthill would kill them in a few days. I tried both methods, on two separate hills. Neither of them worked for my persistent and quite separate anthills. Later my husband went out and bought ant powder. The big gun...an insecticide called diatomaceous earth. It worked.

If you have ants in a vegetable garden and they are undermining your success I know diatomaceous earth will work. It is made of sharp dead and fossilized bodies of diatoms. Keep in mind it's a broad-spectrum insecticide and dangerous if inhaled.

Real Vegetable Gardeners Don't...

Real vegetable gardeners don't begrudge time spent maintaining the garden.

That's because it's an opportunity to check for bugs, scan crops, and enjoy the garden.

Real vegetable gardeners don't get carried away with external inputs.

Remember our guff-busting advice to you way back in the introduction: just ask why.

When it comes to gardening supplies, ask yourself why you need a product—and why it's superior to other products.

There's a lot of greenwashing out there. And lots of advertisements to make gardeners believe they need all sorts of external inputs. Some "organic" or "natural" or "biodegradable" products are great—some are a waste of money.

She said It's far wiser for home gardeners to focus on local suppliers and pesticide-free growing than to jump into the orgy of "natural" and "organic" products on the market.

He said Here's a good example: biodegradable pots. Sure they biodegrade quickly, but that also means you must replace them with new pots every year. I can reuse plastic pots year after year...and I suspect not only does that cost me less money, it probably uses fewer resources too.

Real vegetable gardeners don't fret about a bit of pest damage on their crops.

Sometimes it's not a big deal: a slug-hewn window in some leafy veg doesn't hurt anyone; and a bunch of carrots with occasional carrot fly larva tunnels can have the yucky parts removed.

And doing so is a good lesson for kids, who would otherwise see only the perfect veg in the supermarket.

Summary: Garden Maintenance

The number-one defence against weeds and pests and weak plants is strong soil. Some farmers plant soil-building cover crops (such as fall rye or oats and beans and barley) as part of a pest- and weed-management strategy.

Steven and Donna use compost they make themselves to doctor their soils. Donna also buys inputs such as kelp and fish fertilizer because she believes they will enrich her soil flora. She also likes to brew a batch of compost tea a few times a season to multiply the good bacteria in her worm castings and spread it around a bit.

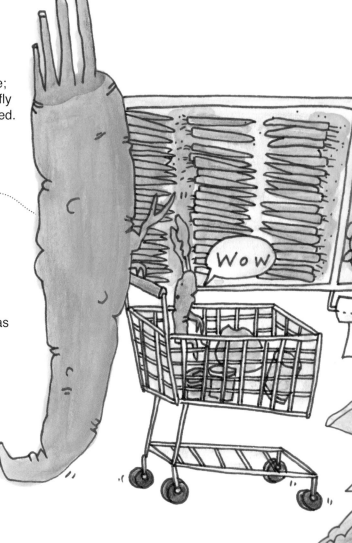
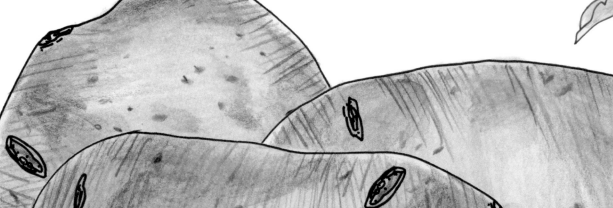

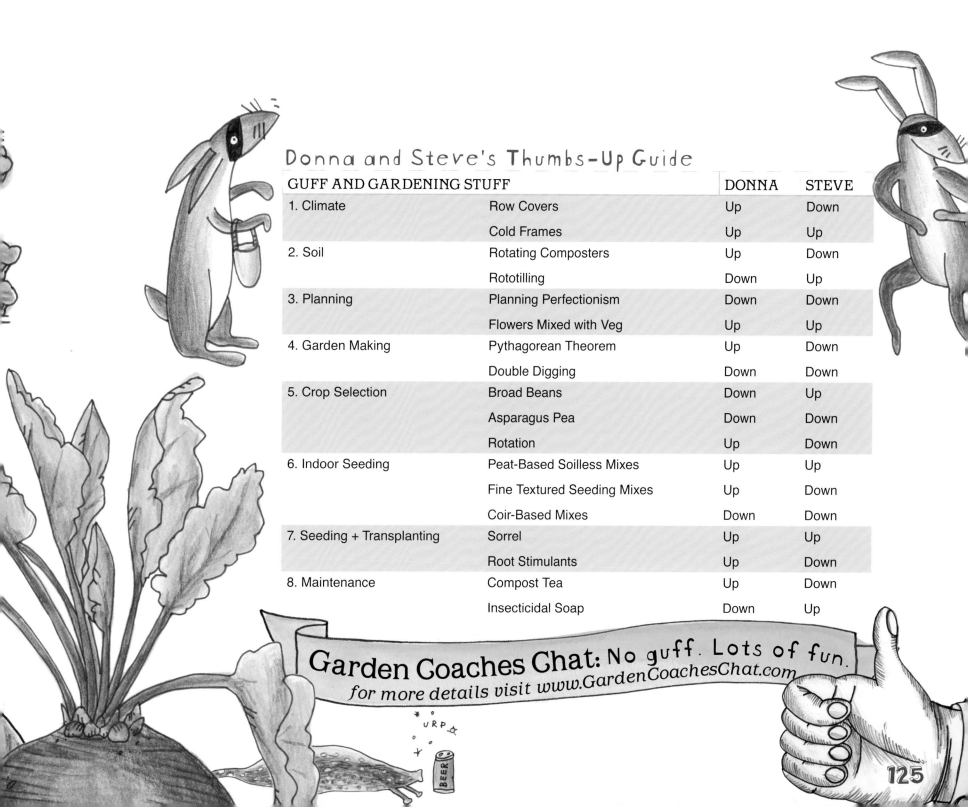

Donna and Steve's Thumbs-Up Guide

GUFF AND GARDENING STUFF		DONNA	STEVE
1. Climate	Row Covers	Up	Down
	Cold Frames	Up	Up
2. Soil	Rotating Composters	Up	Down
	Rototilling	Down	Up
3. Planning	Planning Perfectionism	Down	Down
	Flowers Mixed with Veg	Up	Up
4. Garden Making	Pythagorean Theorem	Up	Down
	Double Digging	Down	Down
5. Crop Selection	Broad Beans	Down	Up
	Asparagus Pea	Down	Down
	Rotation	Up	Down
6. Indoor Seeding	Peat-Based Soilless Mixes	Up	Up
	Fine Textured Seeding Mixes	Up	Down
	Coir-Based Mixes	Down	Down
7. Seeding + Transplanting	Sorrel	Up	Up
	Root Stimulants	Up	Down
8. Maintenance	Compost Tea	Up	Down
	Insecticidal Soap	Down	Up

Garden Coaches Chat: No guff. Lots of fun.
for more details visit www.GardenCoachesChat.com

URP

BEER

HARVESTING AND SUCCESSION CROPS

Ah, the harvest! While a well-planned and grown garden might give you images of a bountiful Thanksgiving harvest, it often doesn't happen that way—especially if you have a small space. In the same way that many businesses have succession plans for executive positions, so too can gardeners—except instead of slotting people into executive roles, gardeners slot crops into vacant or soon-to-be vacant spots in the garden.

Ground left sitting with a spent crop—or bare ground—means lost opportunity: it means sunlight going to waste. The logic behind growing succession crops in the home garden is simple: In a home garden, growing space is often too precious to sit unused.

Succession cropping (sometimes called double cropping) is simply growing a series of crops in the same space. When one crop is finished, the area is used to grow another crop, keeping bare earth to a minimum. Think of turnips planted in August to fill the spot previously occupied by garlic, or July-sown broccoli staking a claim to the former spinach patch.

While the idea of repeatedly replanting may strike some as a lot of work, smaller gardens can usually be quickly planted. And there's another benefit too: keeping a continuous leaf canopy in the garden helps to shade out weeds and feed microbes. (More roots means more root material exuded by roots to feed microbes.)

Not sure what to do with that hole in your garden? Don't leave the soil naked. Plant a cover crop of fall rye (it doesn't have to be fall), or a mixture of field crops sold at farm supply centres. Donna has used rye and a mix of rye and peas. We were told by one grower that buckwheat boosts phosphorus levels in the soil. When the crop is well up, you can turn it under or leave it until spring and then turn it in.

 She said

I'm just too disorganized to be successful with a full slate of succession crops. Maybe that will change as I retire. Meanwhile I have learned to fill the gaps with fall rye.

Top 3 Sensible Harvest and Succession Tips

1. If you're not sure whether a crop is ready or not, pick some and taste it.

2. Check regularly so you don't miss something...or so the critters don't get it.

3. Don't sweat dates: Planting windows for most succession crops are not cast in stone.

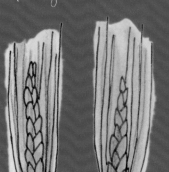

Harvest Tips by Crop

CROP	START PICKING	WHEN MATURE	TOO LATE	INCIDENTALLY
Artichoke (globe)	Flower heads are large enough to be worth harvesting.	Flower head has attained full size, but petals are still tight.	When purple petals start to appear.	Prune off just below the flower bud when harvesting, and smaller side buds may form.
Arugula	As soon as the leaves are big enough to eat.	Leaves become more highly serrated.	When plants bolt (go to seed) and leaves become leathery.	We've heard that some European chefs prefer it with flea beetle holes.
Asparagus	You won't want to wait…but give newly planted crowns a year or two to build up strength before harvesting. As spears emerge, they can be cut off with a sharp knife just below the ground.	Usually when 15–30 cm (6–12 inches), although length and width vary.	When plant has been harvested for four to six weeks, leave it to grow and restore itself for the next season. In the first few years, only pick a few weeks before allowing it to rest.	Stems are ready to pick at various widths from chopstick to thumb size across.
Beans (broad)	If cooking the pod with beans, pick when small.	When beans inside pod have reached a good size.	Pods start to shrivel. At this point, you can start to treat your beans more like a dry bean.	Some people report eating shoot tips too—but we haven't tried that…yet.
Beans (dry)	Don't try to use as a wax bean as many varieties are stringy.	Shells dry.	Shells begin to shatter and beans fall into garden.	There's a bug called a weevil that may have laid eggs on your beans…and weevils can emerge while you store the beans, leaving behind a hole. Place dry beans in oven on cookie sheet at 80 C (180 F) for 15 minutes before storing.

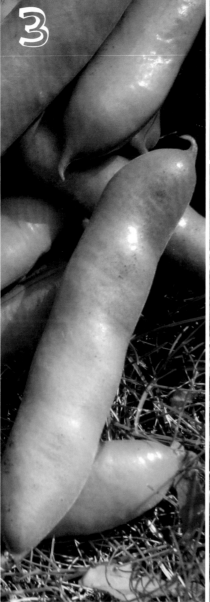

Clockwise from top left:
(1) artichoke ready to pick; (2) asparagus;
(3) broad bean; (4) beet leaves;
(5) Graffiti, a coloured cauliflower;
(6) plump beet root; (7) bush beans;
(8) arugula in flower; (9) artichoke too late.

CROP	START PICKING	WHEN MATURE	TOO LATE	INCIDENTALLY
Beans (bush, pole)	As soon as pods appear and are big enough to be worthwhile picking.	Pods snap easily, but seeds are just visible and not swelling too much.	Bean seeds in the pods become large and visible. Pods get stringy and corky. Save these for harvesting as seed or use as dry beans.	Lift up leaves when picking as beans are often hidden underneath.
Beets	Thin early and use leaves in salads. (If you are worried about kidney stones, don't eat beet leaves.)	Root size varies by variety.	Not an issue in same season. Can be picked well into fall.	Pick beets of the same size, which will require the same cooking time.
Broccoli & Cauliflower	When heads are a decent size.	Florets are closely bunched. Creamy white head for cauliflower.	Broccoli florets (flowers) start to open, revealing yellow petals and heads become loose. Cauliflower heads become loose and are no longer compact.	Slice off broccoli heads, leaving the plant to send up side shoots.
Brussels Sprouts	When bottom sprouts are an inch or so across.	The length of the stalk is covered in well-sized sprouts.	When plants have frozen and fallen over into the mud.	No need to pick all the sprouts at once.
Cabbage	When heads are round and firm. Size varies with variety and location.	Hand squeeze. If firm and not full of soft leaves, it is ready to pick.	Top leaves roll back and head cracks.	If all heads are ready at once, twist some while in ground (a half turn) to prolong harvest window.

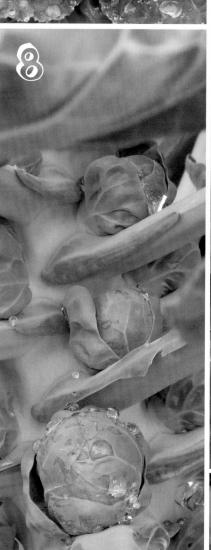

Clockwise from top left:
(1) perfect broccoli; (2) top of Brussels sprouts plant should to be pinched out; (3) Garaflex cabbage; (4) typical ball-head cabbage; (5) Vantage Point cabbage; (6) Marriot loose-head cabbage; (7) rapini, a cousin of broccoli; (8) Brussels sprouts forming; (9) bee on broccoli flower.

CROP	START PICKING	WHEN MATURE	TOO LATE	INCIDENTALLY
Cardoon	One leaf at a time, from the bottom.	Normally these are grown as a perennial in warmer climates and will get bitter late in the season. When grown in cooler climates as an annual, they are good until fall frost.	When the plant flowers.	Once you start picking bottom leaves, a strong wind can cause those above to fall down. Try tying leaves to stem lightly with decorative raffia or rough string.
Carrot	Harvest baby carrots when thinning plants. This leaves the remaining carrots more space to fill out.	Size at maturity depends on variety. Taste best after a light frost.	After the ground freezes hard, texture changes and carrots become mealy or woody. Mulch ground with fall leaves to delay ground from freezing.	Split forked roots when washing to get off all of the soil.
Celery (root)	No point starting too early, just leave it until fall.	The root has reached a size that makes it worthwhile preparing.	Consistency changes after the ground freezes hard.	Will store for a long time in the fridge.
Celery (stalk + leaf)	Donna cheats by picking the outside stalks when she needs celery for soups or other recipes.	When stalks are large enough to harvest.	When plant slumps over. Oops—you've let it freeze solid.	As freezing weather sets in, dig up a couple of plants to keep growing in a cold cupboard, garage, or heated shed and prolong harvest for a couple of months.
Corn	When silk is dry, start checking for ripeness.	When a pierced kernel exudes a milky liquid.	Kernels become starchy and doughy.	After picking, sugars continue to change to starch. Plunge in icy cold water to slow the process.

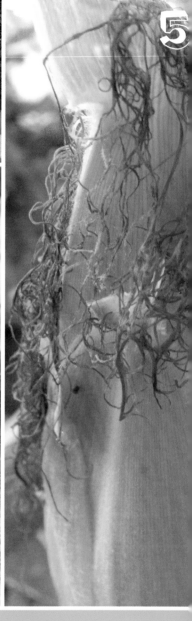

Clockwise from top left:
(1) bok choy (often called pak choy);
(2) container-grown carrots; (3) Quinn's carrots;
(4) celery; (5) corn is ready when female flowers
dry; (6) celery root; (7) dark coloured carrots;
(8) cardoon is very ornamental; (9) young bok choy.

CROP	START PICKING	WHEN MATURE	TOO LATE	INCIDENTALLY
Corn Salad (mâche)	When leaves are big enough to pick.	Nicely formed rosette of leaves.	Plant goes to seed.	Lasts well into cold weather.
Cucumber	Whenever the cucumber is large enough to be worthwhile picking.	Size at maturity depends on variety.	Yellowing indicates that cucumbers are overripe (with the exception of yellow varieties). Larger cukes often have more seeds and start to go spongy in the middle.	Don't worry if the cucumber is curled instead of straight—this just indicates uneven pollination or an insect pest called thrips (which won't harm the eating quality).
Dill	When needed.	Flowers are open and yellow.	Gone to seed.	Save seeds for use in cooking.
Eggplant	As soon as the fruit is large enough to be worthwhile picking. This is a heat-loving plant so it rarely gets too big in cooler climates.	Size at maturity depends on variety. Skin looks like new car leather: firm and glossy.	When left too long, seeds become larger, skin becomes dull, and spots may appear on the skin.	Mind the prickles on the green cap above the eggplant when harvesting. Easier to harvest with scissors than by hand.
Fennel	If bulb is the desired portion, you have to wait, but can pick ferny foliage as a garnish.	When the bulb reaches desired size.	Plant flowers.	Flowers are edible too.

Clockwise from top left:
(1) corn salad; (2) cucumber; (3) white eggplant;
(4) fennel flowers; (5) bulb-like Florence fennel;
(6) purple eggplant; (7) eggplant flower;
(8) young dill leaves; (9) dill seed head.

CROP	START PICKING	WHEN MATURE	TOO LATE	INCIDENTALLY
Garlic	Pick curling, flower-like scapes for use in salads or fast fry.	Mid-summer, tops start to die back and become brown, and bulbs can be dug.	After protective paper covering rots.	Stop watering a few weeks before harvest to allow stalks to dry naturally.
Kale	Take lower leaves as needed, even when plant is smallish.	Leaves can be an arm's length when mature.	Plant freezes solid and dies.	Blooms in second year are tasty but the rest of the plant is not edible when in bloom.
Kohlrabi	When 5–8 cm (2–3 inches) in diameter.	Gradually increases in size.	Becomes tough and woody, and hollow in the centre.	Purple and green varieties available.
Leeks	As soon as the leeks are big enough to be worthwhile preparing. Baby leeks are a nice mid-summer treat.	Can take too long to mature (have a thick stalk) which may mean picking when not fully thickened in areas with a short growing season.	Don't worry if you don't get them all picked in the fall. You can pick a few during a mid-winter thaw or in a mild climate with good snow cover they may overwinter.	Later is better, but enjoy a few baby leeks over the summer too.
Lettuce	As soon as the leaves are large enough to pick, steal a few outer leaves.	Varies by variety—some form heads, some don't. If it is a "leaf-style" lettuce it can be picked early with scissors.	When plants get tall and flower, leaves become bitter.	For head lettuce, cut off at the base instead of pulling out by roots so that the base can send up new shoots.

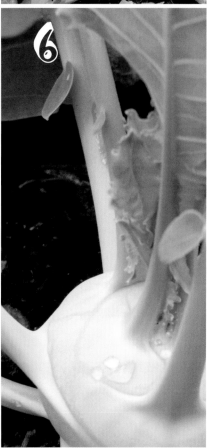

Clockwise from top left:
(1) garlic growing with hay mulch;
(2) mature garlic scape with bulbils ready to plant;
(3) kale gone to seed; (4) kohlrabi;
(5) leeks; (6) kohlrabi close-up; (7)Redbor kale;
(8) field of mixed kale; (9) garlic harvest.

CROP	START PICKING	WHEN MATURE	TOO LATE	INCIDENTALLY
Okra	As soon as pods are big enough to pick.	About 8 cm (3 inches) long.	Once pods get too big, they become woody.	Hard to pinch off by hand, so bring your scissors.
Onions	See onion chart, page 58.			
Parsnips	Don't bother pulling any till after a frost sweetens them.	When the root is big enough to eat.	In cold climates, pick before the ground freezes solid or it will be woody and corky. In mild climates allow these to stay in ground over winter and dig as they are needed.	Leaves may cause allergies when handled with bare skin on a sunny day, a condition called phytophotodermatitis.
Parsley	When the leaves are big enough to eat, they're big enough to pick.	The plant has a full crown of leaves.	When deeply buried with snow. As a biennial, parsley won't flower until its second season.	Continue to pick after the first couple of light snowfalls of the winter season.
Peas (snap + snow)	Sweet to eat any time once pods are growing.	With snow peas, the pod has fully lengthened but is still flat. With snap peas, pods are fat when ready.	For snap peas, once peas inside become hard and mealy.	Pick tendrils and shoot tips as garnishes.

Clockwise from top left:
(1) mixed baby lettuce; (2) okra;
(3) onion ready to harvest;
(4) freshly dug parsnips; (5) perfect snow pea;
(6) braided onions are easy to store;
(7) young onion; (8) mizuna; (9) mixed lettuce.

CROP	START PICKING	WHEN MATURE	TOO LATE	INCIDENTALLY
Peas (shelling)	If you want baby peas, pick when peas are barely visible through pod.	Pods are plump and firm.	Pods lose their sheen and get a yellowish hue. Peas taste hard and starchy.	It's normal for plants to die by mid-summer.
Peppers	When peppers are a worthwhile size. Will be green when immature.	Size and colour at maturity depend on variety.	Fruit will begin to soften and rot. Seeds inside may turn black.	Hard to pinch off by hand, so bring your scissors.
Potatoes	Steal a few early potatoes by feeling around just under the soil surface around the time the plants begin to bloom.	Harvest after foliage dies in mid to late summer.	Ground frozen hard.	Dry in open air for a day…but keep out of direct sun or toxin forms. Store without washing.
Radishes	When radishes are of a size worth picking.	Size and colour depend on variety.	As plant starts to bolt (go to seed), root becomes corky and hot.	Some people like to crunch on the seed pods, which make a great garnish.
Sorrel	Pick leaves all summer.	Leaf size depends on variety.	Good into fall.	Pinch out flower stalks to encourage leaf growth.

Clockwise from top left:
(1) tiny peas in a pod; (2) Emma picks peas;
(3) colourful radish roots;
(4) potatoes grown in leaves are clean at harvest;
(5) radish pods are crunchy and spicy;
(6) edible radish flowers; (7) potatoes grown in soil
yield more than those grown in leaves;
(8) peppers come in many forms and colours;
(9) peas in pods.

141

CROP	START PICKING	WHEN MATURE	TOO LATE	INCIDENTALLY
Spinach	As soon as the leaves are large enough to pick. Use scissors or a sharp knife to get right into the plant and clip out individual leaves.	Leaves usually have rounded or arrowhead shape. Flavour is almost sweet.	Leaves become leathery as plant suddenly gets tall and goes to seed.	There are many tasty substitutes for spinach, see chart, page 59.
Squash (summer) See page 54	Start by harvesting the edible flowers. Can pick very small for use as garnishes.	In zucchini the ideal size is 15–25 cm long (6–12 inches). Pattypan summer squash can be from 5–25 cm (2–10 inches) across.	Skin thickens and seeds become large when left too long.	Will not store as long as winter squash. If squash get big by accident, stuff and bake or grate to include with pasta, quiche, cake, and muffins.
Squash (winter)	Start by harvesting the edible flowers.	Skin should be firm enough that a fingernail won't dent it. The colour becomes duller as the fruit becomes ready to harvest.	Heavy frost can reduce storage quality.	Ten days of curing in a warm spot will help winter squash store longer. Store in dry, cool spot.
Swiss Chard	As soon as the leaves are large enough to pick.	Plant has thick stalks and large leaves.	It's not usually too late in same season, but mature leaves and stalks require longer cooking.	Ribs from large leaves are a good homegrown substitute for bamboo shoots.
Tomatillo	When paper husk loosens and fruit is still pale green.	Taste is best when fruit is pale green.	Fruit begins to yellow and flavour changes.	Plants will get tall or can be left to ramble on ground.

Clockwise from top left:
(1) squash flowers are edible;
(2) sink full of summer squash;
(3) Tiger summer squash; (4) spaghetti squash;
(5) immature tomatillo;
(6) Donna's grandson Cohen picks a pumpkin;
(7) Turk's Turban winter squash;
(8) colourful Swiss chard;
(9) Bloomsdale spinach ready to pick.

143

CROP	START PICKING	WHEN MATURE	TOO LATE	INCIDENTALLY
Tomatoes	Pick green for fried green tomatoes.	Size and colour at maturity depend on variety. There will be gel around the seeds inside the fruit.	Too late if the fruit freezes.	Pick every green tomato before the frost. Layer green tomatoes on newspaper in single layers on a cool basement floor.
Turnip + Rutabaga	2–6 cm (1–3 inches) is a good size for tender, young turnip.	The root becomes plump. Colour depends on variety. Tastes better after a light frost.	The following season the turnip will bolt and bloom if left in the ground over winter.	Try wilted turnip greens as a side dish.

He said My friend Carmen told me that when she grew up on a farm, with a large garden, her family used to wash the carrots in the washing machine. So...despite pained looks from my wife Shelley, I have run a few fall harvests of parsnips and carrots through the wash (no detergent of course).

She said I did not start eating kale until my son cooked it for me a few years ago but now I'm an addict. I love it steamed lightly with lemon and butter. So simple.

He said My wife Shelley has never looked at kale the same way after I accidentally served her steamed caterpillars with the steamed kale one evening.

Clockwise from top left:
(1) Steve's daughter Emma with a tomato selection;
(2) Ruby is a new hybrid cherry tomato;
(3) Turnips are ready to pick in fall.

144

He said My wife and kids make strange faces when served turnip...it's a tough flavour to mask.

My mom, Joanne, talks about Dido and Baba's small market garden in BC—and all the picking she had to do as a child. At the time, she resented it. But now, she's the most thorough bean, pea, and strawberry picker I know. When we would pick as kids, she made sure we used our hands to lift leaves and rifle through plants so we didn't miss a single bean, pea, or strawberry.

I remember growing kale as a kid and thinking it was quite disgusting. Luckily, my Nana thought otherwise and was pleased to take it.

Planning (or Not) for Succession

Succession in the garden isn't about bloodlines or thrones: it's about ongoing planting to give an ongoing harvest. Along with planned succession crops, there are always ample opportunities for unplanned succession crops—even for experienced gardeners. These opportunities arise from seeds that don't come up or crops that fall prey to pests and diseases.

He said Last year my pepper plants were off to a painfully slow start. It was a very cool year—and I was late starting the plants indoors. I knew from experience that there was little chance they'd produce much of a crop before frost. So I yanked them out—and planted arugula in their place.

Starting Succession Crops

Depending on the crop, it may be possible to plant it directly in the garden. But sometimes it's best to have transplants of succession crops underway for when space in the garden becomes available.

Depending on the crop and the location, you can plant directly, use a seedling bed in the garden, or plant in pots. Just remember that hot, dry summer weather can quickly scorch seedlings. It's important to keep them well watered.

aieeeee

She said If you have less than three months of frost-free weather...why bother?

Suitable Crops for Succession

Pick Quick Growers

The second crop—the succession crop—is usually a quickly maturing crop such as beans, lettuce, radishes, spinach, or turnip. Bush beans are an example of a good candidate for succession cropping as they mature quickly and bear a heavy crop over a short period. Spinach, which may bolt or go to seed early because of long days, is best planted in late summer so it can produce in the fall.

Think Twice About Heat Lovers

Succession cropping is less suited to heat lovers such as eggplant, melons, and tomatoes. That's fine, because once they start producing, they continue for quite a while. But it is sometimes possible to fit in an early crop of something like spinach or arugula before setting out late-planted, heat-loving crops after the last spring frost.

Don't Pick Long Season Crops

Long-season crops such as celery, leeks, and parsnips are unsuited to succession cropping as they're in the ground too long to allow time for a second crop.

Steve's 10 Thumbs-up Succession Crops

Arugula   Beets

Broccoli + Cauliflower

Bush Beans   Dill

Endive + Escarole

Kale   Radishes

Rapini

Rutabaga + Turnip

Visit www.GardenCoachesChat.com for more information on these succession crops.

> *She said* This summer I tried succession planting, seeding radishes after I harvested pot-grown potatoes in mid-August. We eventually tried eating the leaves in November, but radish roots never formed even though we got a record long frost-free fall.

GENDER ROLES AFFECT SQUASH HARVEST

She said

On any given squash plant you will find both male and female flowers. Male flowers have thin stems, while female ones have a small, squash-like bulge at the base. No baby-squash bulge? It's a male blossom.

Poorly pollinated female flowers may start growing but the flower falls off before fully developing. When pollinators are in short supply—or if the season has been cold—use a small paintbrush to move pollen from the male flowers onto the female ones.

Many gardeners eat squash flowers. If that's your plan, squash sex education comes in handy: pick only male flowers, leaving a few for pollination.

> **He said** I've never hand-pollinated my squash. I do like to bread and fry the blossoms.

leaves in early July and miraculously he would get a bigger, earlier harvest. While it is true that stress will hasten ripening, it has to be done later in the season when the tomatoes are formed.

Leaves can be removed as part of normal pruning during the season if the plants are the staking type but this will reduce overall yield of tomatoes. If you stop watering in the last few weeks before fall frost, this will also stress plants and promote ripening without all the work. Be careful not to do it too early.

Harvest and Succession Guff Busted

Guff Says

Remove tomato leaves early on to speed ripening.

Guffawers Respond

> *She said* I'm not sure how this rumour got started but I was asked this question by an experienced gardener. He had heard something on the radio and got the impression he could take off all his tomato

Guff Says

Tomatoes must be sprayed with water or hand pollinated with a brush to fruit.

Guffawers Respond

Insect pollinators will take care of your tomato pollination. Encourage local mason bees and honeybees by growing flowers.

> **He said** When I worked in the greenhouse industry, greenhouse tomato growers used either bumblebees or hand-held vibrating tomato pollinators to ensure pollination. This extra pollinating power is needed in the greenhouse environment, where there aren't naturally occurring pollinators.

Harvesting and Succession

Q A

What if I don't have a succession crop?

She said That's fine, but just make sure that you don't have weeds that are going to seed. Instead, sprinkle seeds of a green manure.

My pumpkins are only producing a few female flowers. Why?

Cool evenings. The ladies—the female flowers—come out in greater number when it's warm. You may need to cover the plants at night with plastic to keep the heat up. Remember, adding extra organic matter or fresh compost to soil helps boost heat, because as bacteria finish up the composting task, they give off heat.

Real Vegetable Gardeners Don't...

Real vegetable gardeners don't feel any remorse yanking out a crop that is largely spent.

That's because they see the opportunity to fit in a succession crop.

Real vegetable gardeners don't worry about veg with blemishes.

Instead, the same way they overlook the mole on the nose of their favourite aunt, they overlook the imperfections on homegrown veg.

Cracked tomatoes? Who cares. Lettuce with a resident slug? Get over it.

Summary: Harvesting and Succession Crops

If you can squeeze in one extra batch of peas or full crop of spinach after the early peas are out, you have done something extra. If you can't schedule being home to seed and water that extra crop, at least add a little compost or filler crop of greens to the vacant spot so it will get a boost for the next year.

GUFF AND GARDENING STUFF		DONNA	STEVE
1. Climate	Row Covers	Up	Down
	Cold Frames	Up	Up
2. Soil	Rotating Composters	Up	Down
	Rototilling	Down	Up
3. Planning	Planning Perfectionism	Down	Down
	Flowers Mixed with Veg	Up	Up
4. Garden Making	Pythagorean Theorem	Up	Down
	Double Digging	Down	Down
5. Crop Selection	Broad Beans	Down	Up
	Asparagus Pea	Down	Down
	Rotation	Up	Down
6. Indoor Seeding	Peat-Based Soilless Mixes	Up	Up
	Fine Textured Seeding Mixes	Up	Down
	Coir-Based Mixes	Down	Down
7. Seeding + Transplanting	Sorrel	Up	Up
	Root Stimulants	Up	Down
8. Maintenance	Compost Tea	Up	Down
	Insecticidal Soap	Down	Up
9. Harvest and Succession	Succession Crops	Down	Up

Garden Coaches Chat: No guff. Lots of fun.
for more details visit www.GardenCoachesChat.com

147

CONCLUSION

If you didn't have it before reading the book, we hope you have now caught the vegetable gardening bug. And if you have it, please infect as many people as you can. More than a source of healthy food, vegetable gardening is a lot of fun.

You can spend money on gadgets or inputs, or you can grow without buying very much at all. The main thing is to get your soil in shape. Kids raised in strife-filled households aren't always well adjusted; and plants raised in the war zone of a barren soil are no different.

There's no single right way to garden. Donna does things differently from Steve… and by reading our comments you've probably gathered that. A healthy dose of common sense will take you a long way in the vegetable garden.

There are practices that are wrong or simply don't make sense. We've used Guff to share some of them with you. Keep your eye open for Guff. He'll gladly give you silly advice or point you towards products you simply don't need.

Please tell us about how you inspire new vegetable gardeners at www.GardenCoachesChat.com.

Donna, did I really just write a no-guff gardening book with someone who spent $50 raising a crop of lettuce?

You don't know the half of it Steve. I have learned a lot from that lettuce but its true: I still spend way too much growing this and that. It's a hobby for me. Other girls buy shoes. I buy garden gear.

Closing Guff Busted

Guff Says

> Homegrown produce is buggy and gross.

GUFFAWERS RESPOND

Sorry. That's a backyard canard.

Homegrown veggies aren't full of grubs. They are not somehow inferior to perfect-looking store-bought food. Picked on the day it is served—even if it has a few blemishes—homegrown food is grand.

Guff Says

> Growing vegetables in the city is urban agriculture.

GUFFAWERS RESPOND

Sounds a bit pompous to us. We like the term vegetable gardening. There's no need for a term from academia.

Compare yourself to a farmer if you're running a business, but otherwise, remember that you are a vegetable gardener—not an urban farmer.

Garden Coaches Chat: No guff. Lots of fun.
for more details visit www.GardenCoachesChat.com

Garden Index

A

alfalfa pellets 111

amaranth 59

amendment 19
  definition 22

ant *See* pest

aphids 115

artichoke 68
  harvest 128

arugula 53, 59, 68
  frost hardiness 15
  harvest 128

asparagus 53, 56, 68
  frost hardiness 15
  harvest 128

asparagus pea 59
  frost hardiness 15

B

bacteria 22

bark 33

basil
  frost hardiness 15

bean, broad 53, 68
  harvest 128

bean, dry 68
  harvest 128

bean, bush 60, 68
  frost hardiness 15
  harvest 128
  planting date 20

bean, pole 57, 60, 68
  harvest 130

beds 48
  edged raised 49
  raised 48
  unframed 48

beet 68
  frost hardiness 15
  harvest 54, 130
  leaf 59

bioassay 28

blanching 106

blocks 38

bokashi 30

borax 13

broccoli 68
  frost hardiness 15
  harvest 54, 130

Brussels sprouts 68
  harvest 130

C

cabbage 68
  family 65
  frost hardiness 15
  harvest 130

cabbage root maggot *See* pest

cabbage worm *See* pest

cables, heating 19

cantaloupe
  frost hardiness 15

cardoon 68
  frost hardiness 15
  harvest 132

carrot 57, 70
  frost hardiness 15
  harvest 54, 132

carrot rust fly *See* pest

cauliflower 70
  frost hardiness 15
  harvest 130

celery 70
  frost hardiness 15
  harvest 54, 132

celery root 70
  harvest 132

cell packs 80

chard *See* Swiss chard

cheater row 20

Chinese cabbage
frost hardiness 15

cilantro
frost hardiness 15

climate and weather 14
frost 14, 15
frost hardiness 15
microclimate 16
zone maps 14

cloches and hotcaps 18

coir 91

cold frame 17, 103

cold-temperature injury 15

compost 27
activators 28
greens and browns 27
in-garden 31
leaf 29
leaves to avoid 29
municipal compost 35
pile 30, 171
system comparison 30
tea 106
vermicomposting 31

composter
rotating 30

containers 79

corn 70
frost hardiness 15
harvest 132

corn salad 59, 70
harvest 134

cress
frost hardiness 15

crop rotation 65

crop selection 52
climate 64
early spring start 53
harvest after the first fall frost 54
must-haves 54
no-sweat 60
onion clan 58
perennial vegetables 56
spinach subs 59
squash 55
wow guests 57

crumb rubber 33

cucumber 70
frost hardiness 15
harvest 134

cucumber beetle *See* pest

cutworms *See* pest

D

dahlia 57

damping off *See* disease

days to harvest 64

digging 35, 47
double 50

dill 53, 70
harvest 134

disease
damping off 78

E

earwigs *See* pest

edging
lumber 49

eggplant 70
frost hardiness 15
harvest 134

endive
frost hardiness 15

F

feeding
commercial fertilizers 110
compost and casting 109
plants 109
soil 109

fence, electric 9

fennel 57, 70
frost hardiness 15
harvest 134

fertilizer 90
  fish 111
  granular 90
  inorganic 90
  natural 90
  organic 90
  slow release 78
  water soluble 90

flea beetle *See* pest

front yards 43

frost 14
  average first fall 14, 54
  average last spring 14, 81, 97
  killing 15

fulvic acids 111

fungi 22

fungus, beneficial 31

fungus gnats *See* pest

G

garden-making 46

garlic 53, 72
  frost hardiness 15
  harvest 136

germination 78

GMO 61

greenhouse 20

ground cherries 57

guff
  bean planting dates 20
  beer 123
  blend kitchen waste 34
  borax 13
  coir 91
  delayed planting 123
  double digging 50
  homegrown produce 148
  hoses, soaker and drip 11
  hybrid seeds 67
  ladybugs 123
  Latin names 11
  loam 11
  location 21
  lumber edging 49
  May 24 100
  natural balance 122
  natural products 13
  north-south rows 45
  organic fertilizer 12
  overplanting 100
  peat pots 92
  planning 45
  potatoes 34
  raised beds 50
  save the world 12
  seed retailers 67
  sodium 122
  soil tests 10
  soilless mixes 92
  start early 92
  tomato leaf removal 146
  tomato pollination 146
  transplant fertilizer 100
  urban agriculture 148
  vinegar 122
  watering early 122
  worm castings 92

gypsum 111

H

harden off 98

harvest 126
  tips by crop 128

heirloom *See* seed

herbicide 113
  vinegar 113

herbicide contamination
  laboratory tests 33

hoses, soaker and drip *See* guff

hotbed 18, 68

hotcaps 18

humic acid 111

hybrid *See* seed

I

inoculate 28

insecticides 117
  soap 118

insects
  beneficial 119
  pests 115

J

juglone 29

K

kale 72
  frost hardiness 15
  harvest 136

kelp 111

kohlrabi 72
  frost hardiness 15
  harvest 136

L

labels 81

Latin names *See* guff

leaf miner *See* pest

leeks 72
  frost hardiness 15
  harvest 54, 136

lettuce 17, 53, 72
  harvest 136
  frost hardiness 15

lights
  indoors 81
  flourescent 81

lime 111

loam *See* soil

M

maintenance 102
  daily 104
  monthly 104
  spring 103
  thinning 104
  weekly 104

Malabar spinach 59

manure
  animal manure 31
  green manure 32
  hot bed 18, 68
  horse 19

Mexican gherkins 57

microbes 106
  soil 108

microclimate
    See climate and weather

miner's lettuce 59

mizuna 59

molasses 111

mulch 32
  bark 33
  crumb, rubber 33
  definition 22
  inert 33
  plastic 33
  straw and hay 32
  wood chips 33

muskmellon *See* cantaloupe

mycorrhizae 24, 88

N

nematodes 119

New Zealand spinach 59

north-south rows *See* guff

nutrition
  plant 107
  problems 109
  products 111

O

okra 72
  frost hardiness 15
  harvest 138

onion 53, 72
  frost hardiness 15
  harvest 138
  meet the clan 58

onion maggots *See* pest

open-pollinated *See* seed

orach 59

organic *See* seed
certified 12
definition 12
gardening 12
matter 12

P

parsley 41, 72
frost hardiness 15
harvest 54, 138

parsnip 72
frost hardiness 15
harvest 54, 138

peas 53, 74
frost hardiness 15
shelling
harvest 140
snap and snow
harvest 138

peat moss 32

pelleted *See* seed

pepper 74
frost hardiness 15
harvest 140
poor germination 93

perennials 56, 62
timing 94

pest
animal 120
deer 121

rabbits 120
raccoons 120
smaller 121
squirrel 120
barriers, insect 116
control, insect 116
insect
ant 123
cabbage root maggot 115
cabbage worm 115
carrot rust fly 115
cucumber beetles 115
cutworm 115
earwig 115
flea beetle 115
fungus gnats 91
leaf miner 115
onion maggot 115
potato beetle 115
slug 115
spider mites 115
tomato hornworm 115
wireworms 115

planning
access 37
alleys and laneways 44
blocks 38
colour 39
considerations 37
exercise 37
front yard 43
kitchen 41
landscape themes 39
paper 40
precision 38
rows 38
shape 38

size 40
sunlight 38, 42
textures and shapes 39
trees 42
water source 41

pollution
lead 44

potato 34, 74
frost hardiness 15
harvest 140
seed 95

potato beetle *See* pest

pots *See* containers

peat *See* guff

pricking out 86

protozoa 108

psychology
garden 102

pumpkin
frost hardiness 15
See squash, winter

R

radish 53, 74
frost hardiness 15
harvest 140

raised beds 50

rhubarb
forcing 56

frost hardiness 15

rock dust 111

root-trainers 80

rotation
  cabbage family 65
  crop 65
  simplified 66

rototiller 50

row covers 16

rows 38

rutabaga 76
  harvest 144

S

sage
  frost hardiness 15

salts 35, 122
  road 43

screening 96

seaweed 111

seed
  exchanges 64
  genetically modified 61
  germination 97
  heirloom 61
  hybrids 61
  longevity 63
  mail order 64
  open-pollinated 61
  organic 61

pelleted 61
retailers 67
saving 62, 63
spacing 97
starting 95
storing 67
terminology 61
treated 61
untreated 61
viability 73

seeding, indoors 78
  calendar 81
  containers 80
  humidity 85
  labels 81
  large seeds 84
  light 84
  lights and timers 81
  methods 83
  pricking out 87
  soilless mixes 78
  temperature 85
  timing 82
  transplanting 87
  trays 80
  watering 85
  when 82

seeding, outdoors
  drill 96
  early spring 95
  fall 95
  methods 96
  plant parts 94
  scatter 96
  scatter and poke 96
  spacing 97

timing 94
transplanting 94

seedling
  care 88
  feeding 89
  watering 89

self-pollinating 62

shade 42

slug See pest

sod removal 47

soil 22
  abuse 26
  acidic 26
  aggregates 26
  alkaline 26
  amendments 27
  cracked 34
  definition 22
  digging 35
  fungi 26
  loam 11
  microbes 24
  organic matter 23
  particle size 24
  pH 26
  sterilizing 78
  structure 23
  tests 28
  textures 24

soilless mix 78

sorrel 56, 74
  harvest 140

spider mites *See* pest

spinach 17, 53, 74
  frost hardiness 15
  harvest 142
  substitutes 59

squash 74
  family explained 54, 55
  frost hardiness 15
  gender 146
  summer
    harvest 142
  winter
    harvest 142

stakes 107

sterilizing 80

straw and hay *See* mulch

succession crops 95, 145

sulphur 26

sweet potato 60

Swiss chard 59, 74
  frost hardiness 15
  harvest 54, 142

T

tillage
  before seeding 94
  digging 47
  newly cleared soil 47
  rototiller 50

tomatillo 76
  harvest 142

tomato 57, 76
  caging 105
  frost hardiness 15
  harvest 144
  sprawling 105
  staking 105
  transplanting outdoors 98
  trellising 105

tomato hornworm *See* pest

tool
  hand-held seeder 107
  hoe 107
  leaf blower 107

transplant
  definition 60
  harvest-staggering 99
  outdoors 98
  timing 97

transplants
  versus seed-grown 60

treated *See* seed

treated lumber 49

treated seed *See* seed

tunnels 20

turnip 76
  frost hardiness 15
  harvest 54, 144

U

untreated *See* seed

V

veggiephobia 43

vermicomposting 31

vinegar *See* herbicide

volunteer crops 94

W

walled vegetable garden 17

walnut toxicity 42

watering
  morning *See* guff

watermelon
  frost hardiness 15

weather
  data 14

weeds 59, 112
  cultivation 112
  edible 113
  physical barriers 113
  pulling 112

wireworms *See* pest

wood chips *See* mulch

worm bin 30

worm castings 31

zone maps 14

zucchini 54
  frost hardiness 15
  See squash, summer

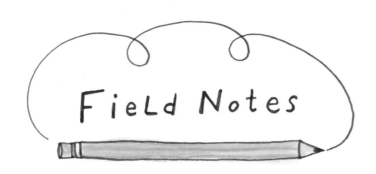

Field Notes

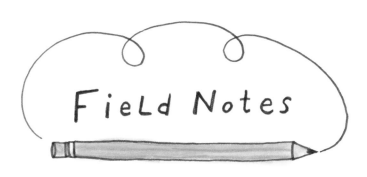

FEEDLOT STUDIOS

www.feedlotstudios.ca

The artistic design team nestled Steve and Donna's words in playful, informative designs that are equally at home on coffee tables, in sophisticated libraries, or on the bookshelves of serious gardeners.

Mariko and Bryan McCrae are the owners and artists of Feedlot Studios on Gabriola Island in B.C. Mariko is an award winning ceramics artist and teacher. Beyond just sketching vegetables, it is her imagination and sense of humour that gave birth to the mischievous rabbit, Ernie McGuff—and to onions in kilts and scallions with mittens. Bryan is a master of corporate brand artistry, web page design, and integration of visual elements. Bryan melds text, art, and photographs into an easy reading composition.

Feedlot Studios is all about promoting and sustaining the arts—both visual and graphic. Their focus is on educating the community by providing workshops and classes. Activities range from ceramic classes for children to web, print and logo design. As this book goes to print, Mariko's prize winning "Willow Tops" ceramic golf shoes are on tour across Canada.

FEED
LOT
studios

ceramic + web and print design